THE SEVEN RAYS
Key to the Mysteries

by

Dr DOUGLAS BAKER
B.A., M.R.C.S., L.R.C.P., F.Z.S.

First published in 1977

'Little Elephant'
Essendon, Herts.
Printed and bound in Great Britain

ISBN 0-906006-69-4

Contents

Part One

THE BASIS OF LIFE

1

Nature of the Seven Rays

The Hylozoistic Theory

The nature of the Seven Rays is inextricably interwoven with the most basic theories of that unequalled classic of occult wisdom, *The Secret Doctrine*. The most prominent of these theories is that of Hylozoism.

Hylo derives from the Greek word for matter, and *-zoism* means life. The theory propounds that *everything* lives – from the tiniest atom to the greatest galaxy. Even today, this theory, which is pantheism taken to its logical conclusion, is anathema to the biologist and even our more earnest students of the esoteric sometimes boggle at it.

Mme Blavatsky's proposition came at a time when science was only just beginning to reject the concept that the basic elements were made up of tiny balls of their respective substances ... a concept which dated back 500 years B.C. to Democritus. The possibility that atoms could contain life, or worse, some degree of sentiency or consciousness, seemed absurd then and the position hardly changed for another twenty-five centuries.

That atoms can be alive may still seem to the scientist a very foolish speculation, but there are signs that a new thinking along these lines may be taking place. The advent of the electron microscope and the influx of enlightened men like Nobel Prize winner, John Howard Northrop, are throwing new light on to the subject.

Northrop declares:

> Today the division between organic and inorganic chemistry has completely disappeared and the mechanisms of a great many of the chemical reactions which occur in living matter are now thoroughly understood.

The barriers are creaking.

Lying between the realm of the cell or of bacteria and that of atoms and molecules, is the enigmatical virus. Outside of a tissue cell, in which it *has* to 'live', the virus turns out to be nothing more than a crystal! The tobacco virus is a typical example. Within the cells of tobacco plants it is able to multiply and grow; it shows many of the accepted characteristics of life. In *The Scientists Speak* (Boni and Gaer, Inc., New York), Northrop remarks:

> Certain proteins, in fact, provide the best possible evidence for the close relationship between chemistry and life. For among the proteins are viruses, those strange and tiny objects which sometimes *act as though they were alive*, and which at other times are pure chemical substances, as inert in a bottle as so much sugar or salt.

Speaking of some other proteins, known as enzymes, Northrop has this to say:

> Two of the enzymes, pepsin and trypsin, possess the extraordinary property of causing their own formation. These enzymes are not present as such, in the body tissues. Instead, there is present, a peculiar protein, which has no effect on any reaction ... if this inert protein is dissolved under certain conditions and a trace of either pepsin or trypsin added, all the inert protein present changes to pepsin or trypsin. These enzymes can therefore reproduce themselves, a property which has frequently been considered a distinguishing characteristic of *living things*.
>
> Thus, the criterion of reproduction, which has been used to distinguish the quick from the dead, has failed, and the problem of defining a living thing, always a difficult one, has become even more difficult. It begins to look as though this difficulty is inherent in the subject, and may be due to the fact that *there exists no fundamental distinction between living and inanimate things*.

And so we see that the teaching of the *Secret Doctrine*, which only elaborates on the same proposition put by Aristotle, is now far more acceptable in the most respectable of scientists today. Weldall M. Stanley, also awarded a Nobel Prize for his work on viruses, admits in *The Scientists Speak* that 'Nature has made such a gradual transition from the non-living to the living, that the boundary is doubtful and probably non-existent.'

Crystals are alive within cells and practising the equivalent of animal hibernation when out of them. Are we not restricted from applying this proposition that all crystals are *all* alive, merely because we lack the scientific know-how to prove it?

The Whole Planet Is Alive

Once we accept that life may exist in even the smallest particles of matter, we must also accept that the whole of the planet is alive. Hylozoism does not stop at the atom; nor does it stop at man. It proposes that atoms live within greater forms than themselves. Some atoms live within the body of the molecule, which we have seen is accepted by many as living. Living molecules sometimes form part of the body of a greater being which is the tissue cell or unicellular organism. Many cells come together to form greater structures like man himself. Each entity, no matter how large or how small, is alive and lives within the body of a greater being somewhere along the scale of evolution.

What lies beyond that living entity which is man? Does he live within the body of a greater being? The Wisdom of the Ages proposes that he is no exception, that man lives within that sentient and great entity which we call a Root Race, at the centre of which is a Manu. And, going even further, the Root Races themselves are not only sensitive living entities, but they form but part of the body of that great, living entity Humanity.

Our Fifth Root Race (whose outward form is so well-known to us who compose it) is, inwardly, a living centre of etheric force in Humanity ... a centre which corresponds to our own throat chakra. And the Atlantean Race, the Fourth, corresponds to the solar plexus centre in that distinguished Being. In the same way, the remnants of Lemuria correspond to the sacral centre, for even in Him, within Whom we live and move and have our being, there is evolution of consciousness, and His is drawing away from His sacral and solar plexus centres and is shifting into that of the throat. Hence the upsurgence of the Fifth Root Race.

And whilst science may laugh over such apparently nonsensical statements, we can wait patiently until that day when it will be intuited by the great masses that even the planets of our solar system and those of others, are but the outward expression of great lives, and so on, right up to the very galaxies themselves. Our Milky Way, the galaxy in which we live, is alive and sentient and has an evolving consciousness governed by the same great laws of Being which rule ourselves and the tiniest atoms.

For centuries, our own solar system has been given the esoteric name of 'The Grand Man of the Heavens' and yet even He is but the heart centre within the body of a far greater being that even the highest initiate can only dimly sense; and it is no wonder that He is referred to as 'The One About Whom Naught May Be Said'.

You will have noticed that we have arrived almost at a consideration of the universal, and this is essentially the occult method: to study the universal as a preliminary to a consideration of the particular, which in this instance is to be man. We are trying to understand something of the stupendous consciousnesses of those great Beings in whom we live before attempting to evolve a psychological formula for ourselves.

One of the great keys to an understanding of such stupendous Beings who make up the consciousness of the Divinity is the sacred science of astrology. Again we find in many esotericists a block, or refusal to admit this essential key to The Secret Doctrine into their scheme of things. This attitude is generally due to laziness or the fear of incurring ridicule in the outside world. The laziness prevents a thorough investigation and testing of the key. Whilst astronomers do magnificent work in unravelling the anatomy of the universe, there is ever room for a physiology to explain the functions of the anatomical parts of the universe. It is astrology, especially *esoteric astrology*, which at the moment performs this function best.

The Endocrine Glands and the Planets

The esotericist will be familiar with the etheric or vital body of man. He will know that there are seven major vortices of etheric energy located in well-known sites of the body. He will also know that overlying these force centres or *chakras* are endocrine glands which have the function of pouring certain hormones or chemical messengers into the gross physical body in order to produce certain specific and generally well-understood results. He will also know that the correct functioning of these glands is, in no small measure, greatly dependent upon the underlying ether body which vitalizes these special organs and which also maintains the integrity of the various nervous systems through small etheric processes called *nadis*.

Whilst there have been many and varied attempts to allocate the planets of our solar system to their respective rulership over the endocrine glands, there is no dispute amongst esotericists over the fact that the planets *do* influence them.

This practice is basic to the occultist and it implies, of course, that man is made in the image of a greater being; he is made in the image of the solar system in which he lives and moves and has his being. In the diagram overleaf we see man as a microcosmic replica of a solar system with planetary symbols positioned over the sites of his endocrine glands and the underlying chakras.

Taking the pattern higher into the macrocosm, the seven sacred planets of the solar system correspond to the endocrine glands and underlying chakras in 'The Grand Man of the Heavens', the name given to the living entity using our solar system as form within which to evolve and to express himself. The Logoi or spiritual entities ensouling these centres are known as the Seven Spirits Before the Throne. Their function is to receive and transmute, as well as to transform, the energies stemming from the Solar Sphere and to apply them in their own planetary systems.

We must go even further, though with each step towards the macrocosm our understanding becomes diminished (as it does when we go into the microcosmic atom). We must begin to speculate on the nature of that stupendous being in Whom our solar Logos is but a chakra. 'The Grand Man of the Heavens', or Solar Logos, corresponds to the heart chakra in 'The One About Whom Naught May Be Said'.

There is other evidence. The great star Sirius, the constellation of the Dragon, The Pleiades, and The Great Bear, are also force centres of equal or greater importance in that Being.

It is taught that the seven stars of The Great Bear represent the seven etherico-physical head centres in 'The One ...' — counterparts of those in our own human brains. The seven stars (one is not visible) of The Pleiades are said to correspond to the Throat Centre in Him. We know that Sirius is to the Sun what Venus is to the Earth ... an alter ego ... probably the Head Centre in 'The One'. The writer would be merely hazarding a guess at the function of the constellation of the Dragon, said to be the most occult of all constellations, but he would place this as a correspondence with the brow chakra or ajna.

Somewhere in this particular plan, the great star Betelgeuse plays a part. But even 'The One About Whom Naught May Be Said' is living within the body of a much greater Being who is the galaxy in which we live and which we call the Milky Way.

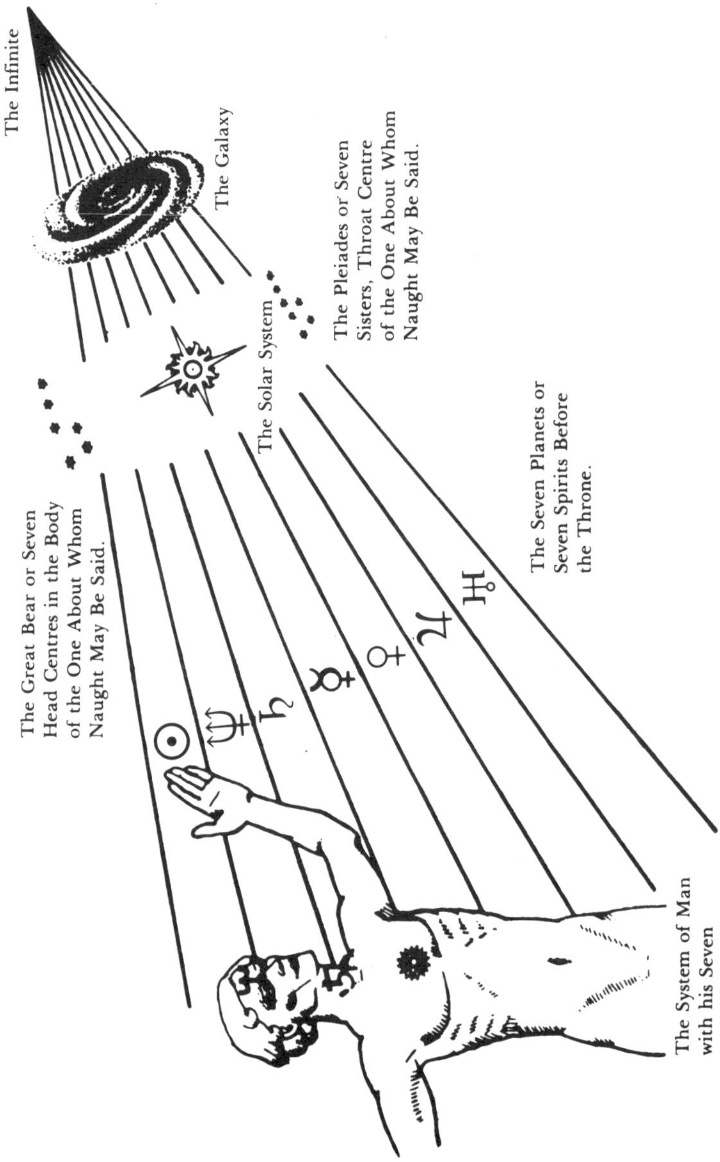
The Infinite
The Galaxy
The Pleiades or Seven Sisters, Throat Centre of the One About Whom Naught May Be Said.
The Solar System
The Great Bear or Seven Head Centres in the Body of the One About Whom Naught May Be Said.
The Seven Planets or Seven Spirits Before the Throne.
The System of Man with his Seven Body Centres.

THE ORIGIN OF THE SEVEN RAYS

THE SYMBOLIC EMERGENCE OF THE MAJOR RAYS

In the right-angled triangle we have the symbol of Spirit in the vertical side; matter is symbolized by the horizontal side and the hypotenuse symbolizes the emergence of the blending of both, i.e. form. The quality of the form is related to these three sides in the three major Rays of Will and Power, Love-Wisdom and Active Intelligence. This is but one of the many meanings behind the 47th theorem of Pythagoras (The Master K.H.).

Origin of the Seven Rays

The drawing opposite depicts the origin of The Seven Rays, arising as they do from the seven stars of The Great Bear (sometimes called The Plough). They are the outward manifestation of the seven head centres of 'The One About Whom Naught May Be Said'. He is using the great Sun Sirius, known as the Dog-star, the star of Mercury and as the star of the Buddha, to focus the light of the Seven Rays (of Logoic Mind) ... as symbolized by the mirror ... on to the Sign of Aquarius and the planet Earth:

From the point of Light within the Mind of God
Let light stream forth into the minds of men.
Let light descend on Earth.

He points (the Finger of God) at the new Age, and energy follows thought. Beneath his beard (concealed by the Wisdom of the Ages) lies the secret of The Pleiades worn as a seven starred necklace overlying His throat centre. Our sun lies over His heart centre and rays out its note of Love-Widsom:

From the point of Love within the Heart of God
Let love stream forth into the hearts of men.
May Christ return to Earth.

The symbol of Earth lies directly in the two streams of energy and contains as its centre the Sign of Christos. The Finger of God has not quite drawn the full Sign of Aquarius, implying that the Age is not yet fully manifest. There is constant interplay between the great zodiacal constellations depicted in the lower ellipse and their ruling planets in the higher one.

Great triangles of energy should have been depicted (but omitted for the sake of simplicity) interacting between, for instance, The Pleiades, Sirius and our sun. This has little meaning until it is translated by Ray correspondences to our own human microcosm which then reveals the powerful human triangle of head, heart and throat centres.

Readers are reminded that the drawing, in no way, attempts to depict God. The Grand Architect of the Universe ever hides Himself beyond the furthermost horizons of even the most enlightened conjecture. Instead, we have attempted to give some sort of synthesizing concept of the origin and overall functions of

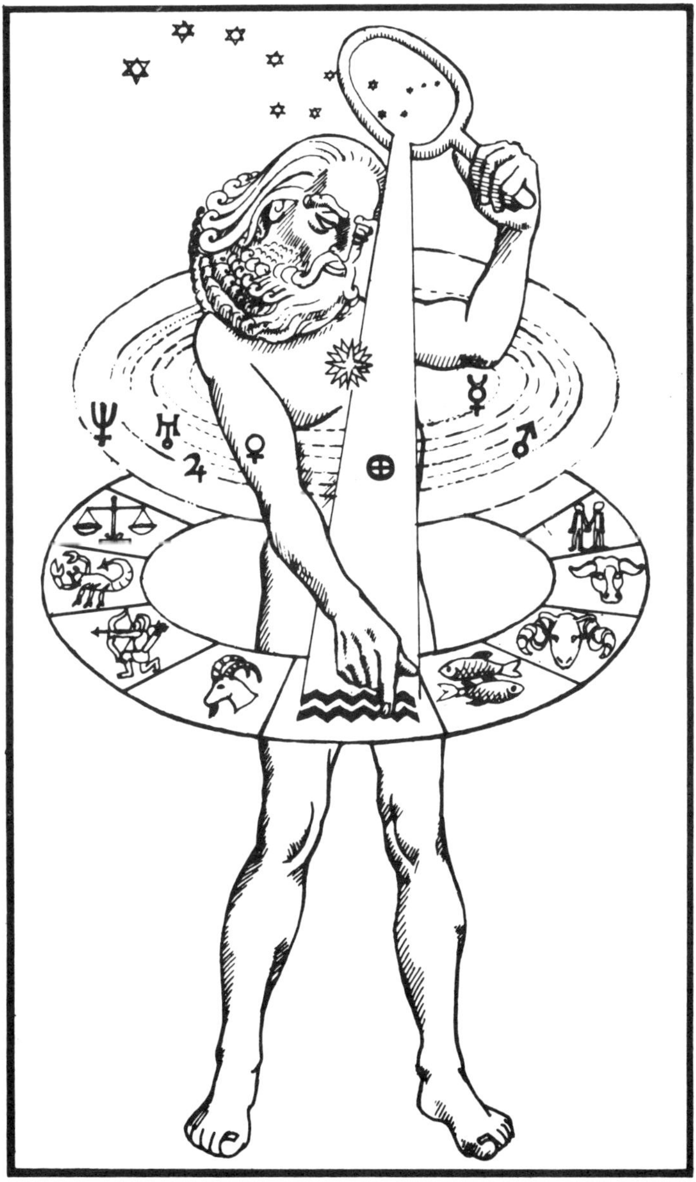

the Seven Rays.

Why then have we made this excursion into what must seem the realms of phantasy, even to the most devout occultist? We have had to search this far in order to locate the *origin* of the Seven Rays, for they represent the Seven Great Qualities permeating the entire nature of 'The One About Whom Naught May Be Said'. They not only stem from there but they are the Seven Builders of any and all the lesser entities contained within Him or of which He is comprised. Nothing exists below His level or amongst the many entities which have been described macrocosmically or microcosmically above, which are not filled with these Seven or fashioned under their influence.

The Seven Rays are not only the Great Builders but they are the custodians of The Plan. They produce the radiant temple of the Lord under the guidance of the mind of the Great Architect of the Universe. All Seven Rays are needed and all are coloured by a divine quality needed for the perfecting of the latent and unrevealed purpose of God.

Our sun, or Solar Logos, is the great channel for the Second of these Seven Rays. He, Himself a heart chakra in the greater being, channels the Ray of Love-Wisdom. The predominant guiding force then, for all within our solar system, is Love wisely applied. All other six Rays are sub-rays to this one in *our* solar system. The colour of the great Ray of Love-Wisdom is indigo, the colour of the sky on a moonless night. The colours of the sub-rays are scarlet, green, yellow, orange, blue, rose-red and violet. We speak of the colour of the First Ray in our solar system as being indigo-scarlet; the Third Ray is indigo-green, etc. The colour of the Second Ray is really, then, indigo-indigo.

Whilst the dominating Ray of our solar system is indigo, that of the Pleiades would be green because it represents the throat chakra in that being which has our solar system as a heart centre, etc. The planet in our solar system which represents the throat centre is Saturn, and its colour is green. The Ray of Saturn is also the Third Ray and there is, then, a special affinity between Saturn, The Pleiades and the human throat centre.

The Work of the Rays

Through manipulation of the Seven Rays, our Solar Logos is able to obtain the endless variations of form within His System. There is nothing in our solar system, at whatever stage of evolution it may stand, which does not belong to the Seven Rays, or respond

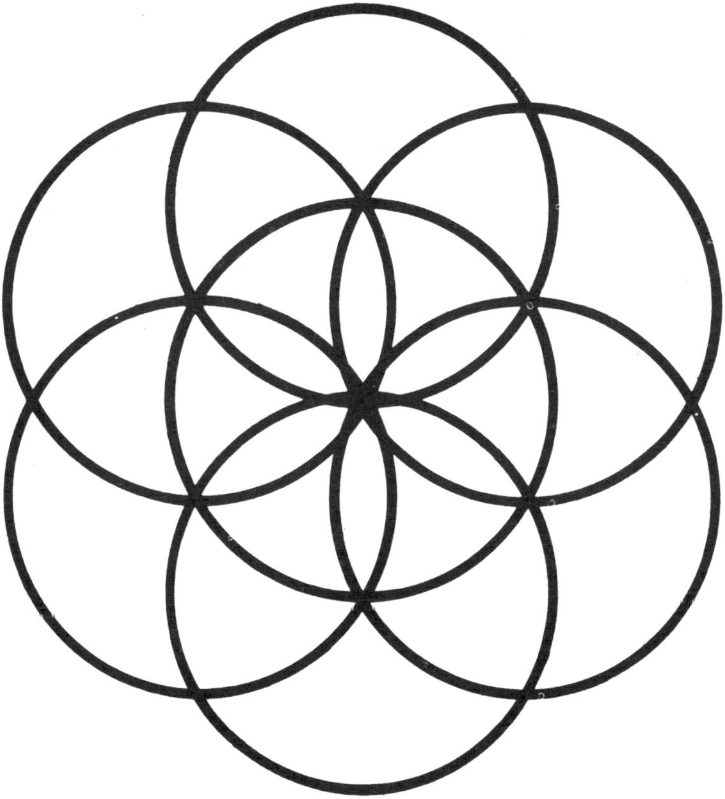

THE SEPTENARY NATURE OF THE CIRCLE

Six satellite circles and the 7th or synthesising one ... the 2nd Ray of Love-Wisdom which embraces all the others.

to the Seven Rays. The Rays flow out from the centre of the sun, from the so-called heart of the sun. They are received into the solar system through the Central Spiritual Sun. They are transmitted to the Seven Spirits Before The Throne, which are the Seven Heavenly Men, or Logoi of the seven sacred planets of our system. Intermingling and blending with each other, according to their missions, they reach the earth through its seven centres. One of these is situated in London; there is one at New York, one at Darjeeling and one at Geneva.

As we have begun to see, each human is a replica of the great plan for the universe and the Seven Rays are the linking and synthesizing qualities which bring all cosmos into relationship with each other and direct them according to the will and plan of the Architect of the Universe. The Seven Rays are, therefore, the embodiments of seven types of force which demonstrate to us the seven qualities of deity whether these be in the form of sound, colour, fragrance, taste or in the host of other manifestations.

The Seven Rays or qualities of the One life pervade the whole universe and yet remain individual and undiminished. As *The Bhagavad Gita* says: 'Having pervaded the entire Universe with a fragment of myself, I remain.' We find references to the Seven Spirits Before The Throne of God in the writings of Plato and all initiates who, in ancient and modern times, laid down basic propositions for the guidance of human mentality down through the ages.

The Pythagorean school of initiates spoke of the Music of the Spheres and they spoke with good reason because each of the Seven Rays emits its own sound and, in so doing, sets in motion those forces which must work in unison with it. The sound or Word of each Ray passes down through the heavens reaching into every solar or planetary sphere on that Ray note, right down into ourselves and the myriad lives of lesser entities who make us up.

The Seven Rays are the Seven Breaths of that One Life and in Him, just as in us, there is an important relationship between breath, sound and thought.

Physical Manifestation of the Rays

If any entity, human, planetary or solar, wishes to create (but not procreate), he does so first in thought substance. Every thought held in the mind is potentized at each in-breathing. Fine energies run through and enliven the delicate thought meshwork. During the moment of out-breathing the mind, if it so wishes, is then best suited to drive the thoughtform forth into manifestation. During this out-breathing, the breath creates or is accompanied by a sound. The sound or note or word attracts to the thoughtform the building devas, the elementals which fashion the atoms and molecules into the final form.

We, our human selves, are steadily built by in-breathing, a very necessary step required to charge the etheric matrix with the energy it needs to build up physical tissue, or to maintain it, or to destroy it.

C.W. Leadbeater, in one of his many valid treatises, showed

how the breath divides up and charges the seven major chakras of the etheric body. Each of the Seven is ruled by a Ray quality which attracts to the vortex devas of the corresponding Ray. Tissue forms in that region, following the etheric matrix, and thenceforth that tissue will respond to the Ray that built it ... an important consideration when the ancient art of healing is employed to assist diseased tissue back towards a state of health.

And so our physical temples are built through Ray influence and are maintained until the last in-breathing. The same holds good for substances on the mental and emotional levels of human manifestation. In understanding the Seven Rays, we therefore come to an important understanding of our real natures at all levels. This is the basis of the psychology of the Seven Rays.

An example of this process is beautifully demonstrated in the evolving embryo where organizing centres have been demonstrated by embryologists. Each of these very real centres in physical substance attracts and organizes matter into tissue. If part of the tissue in that region is destroyed, the organizing centres will rebuild the tissue *into the same shape*. Destroy the centre and no further replacement of identical tissue will take place.

Ray Differentiation

Before studying the effects of the Rays on ourselves, we must first consider some factors in relation to their qualities and differentiation. The three Major Rays are Rays I, II and III. They are:

Ray I The Ray of Will and Power.
Ray II The Ray of Love-Wisdom.
Ray III The Ray of Intelligent Activity.

These three correspond very closely to the Trinity as it is understood in all the religions on this planet, but they are *not* the Trinity itself. They are the first manifestation of the Trinity and by studying some of the descriptions of the Trinity, we are able to gather something of the qualities of these three major Rays and thence come to a better understanding of the four minor Rays which spring from the Three.

First Aspect	**Second**	**Third**
Father	Son	Holy Ghost
Spirit	Form	Matter
Protons	Neutrons	Electrons
Light	Magnetism	Heat

Inertia	Rhythm	Activity
Nitrogen	Oxygen	Hydrogen
Alkali	Salt	Acid
Electric Fire	Solar Fire	Fire by Friction
Siva	Vishnu	Brahma
Tamas	Sattvas	Rajas
Will	Love	Activity

Above are some of the better-known descriptions of the Trinity. The list is as long as is human experience of his environment.

The Second Ray dominates the Second Solar System which is our own present one. The First Ray will dominate the second Solar System's successor, the system that follows this one after the solar pralaya. The Third Ray dominated the last Solar System.

The four remaining Rays are Rays of Attribute and they are products of the Major Three. For instance, Ray Four is a blending of Ray I and Ray II. The following list shows how the Seven Rays arise from an interplay with each other. The possible combinations of the three Major aspects of the Trinity is seven:

1́ – 2 – 3 = Ray I
1 – 2́ – 3 = Ray II
1 – 2 – 3́ = Ray III

An accent is placed over the aspect of the Trinity concerned. The Minor four are made of in the following way:

1́ – 2́ – 3 = Ray IV
1́ – 2 – 3́ = Ray V
1 – 2́ – 3́ = Ray VI
1́ – 2́ – 3́ = Ray VII

It will now be understood that there is apparently some overlapping of the qualities of the Rays but this is because of common derivations.

Ray Cycles

At solar and planetary levels:

In previous manvantaras, matter – physical, emotional and mental – became organized to varying degrees. Pralaya intervenes and then, when the cycle of manifestation returns (the manvantara), the notes of each Ray are sounded forth. The previously organized matter of each particular Ray responds to the Ray once more, or rather to its note, and the building continues. As a Ray influence wanes under cyclic law, another will take up its work according to the Plan.

At human levels:
The Rays are the builders of the entire human entity, of *all* its subtle bodies. They build:

at the Monadic level;
at the level of the Soul, and its higher Triad of bodies;
at the Personality level, and its lower Triad of Physical, Emotional and Mental bodies.

The Rays cycle in and out of manifestation and every human being is swept into incarnation on the impulse of some Ray and the Life and Form are coloured by that Ray quality.

The same applies to *every* animal, plant and mineral.

The Ray of the human Monad continues unchanged through the aeons. There are some 63 thousand million working through our planetary system and they are divided between the three Major Rays only. Some 3 thousand million are on the Ray of Will and Power. The balance are almost evenly divided between the Second and Third Rays.

The Ray of the Soul varies from round to round, and in the more evolved souls from race to race. We thus tend to change the Ray of our Souls as we take up bodies in the Lemurian, Atlantean and Aryan Races. The Ray of the Soul may be any one of the Seven.

At this time, there are relatively few First Ray souls, and even fewer Fourth Ray souls, manifesting. Most of these souls treading the Path are on the Second Ray of Love-Wisdom or (especially Christians) on the Sixth Ray. Under the stimulus of the new Age, Seventh Ray Souls are coming in fast.

2

Seven Ray Psychology

The picture shows symbolically the unveiling of the esoteric psychology of man. Michelangelo's youthful David emerges from the now partly disclosed temple of the Mysteries, supported as it is by the seven columns or the Seven Rays of which almost five manifest at any one time. David symbolizes the eternal youth of seventeen summers, Sanat Kumara, the Logos of this planet.

He is the Lord of the Ageless Wisdom, the Silent Watcher, the Ancient of Days and the hope of Hierarchy. He sallies forth at this time to start a new Age by destroying the Goliath of materialism and to restore the Mysteries on Earth. The skull symbolizes not only the anatomical and physiological paths of science as a means to comprehending man's structure, but also the *inner* man whose real nature called forth the Delphic instruction to all initiates, "Man know thy *self*."

The psychology of the Seven Rays originated in records made from observations of man's behaviour over a period of some eighteen million years on this planet. It is valid for men of all races, creeds, castes, sex and colour. It represents the essence of a divine wisdom or 'Gnosis' won by the blood and sweat of some of the foremost leaders of the human race during their own struggles through many lives against the planetary environment and the forces of involution.

This psychology takes into account a third factor mostly ignored by contemporary psychologists. The other two, more traditional, factors come under the heading of *environment* and *hereditary equipment*. The *third* factor postulates an inner, spiritual nature for man, and it is only recently that it has found some sort of representation in those current schools of psychology which represent the so-called existential approach as exemplified by Professor A.H. Maslow in *Towards A Psychology Of Being*; Frankl; Roberto Assigioli, M.D., in *Psychosynthesis*; and others.

The Seven Rays analyse the anatomy and function of these various units of spiritual energy which constitute the vehicle of expression of man's soul and which constantly stimulate or moderate the elements of man's personality from within, and which he comes to recognize as a 'spiritual conscience'. It is through the effects mainly of this inner nature that man is able to integrate his personality to such an extent that it sounds forth as a single note and is then able to express some of those inner powers said to be latent in man and now being examined by various scientific bodies as extra-sensory perception, parapsychology, etc.

The teachings on the Seven Rays are a key to the true nature of man, embracing all scientific, occult and mystical knowledge, and provide a framework for understanding God's Plan for atom, cell, planet, galaxy – and for Man himself.

The Rays give us new methods of healing, new light on the origin of disease (see my book *Esoteric Healing, I*), and teach the manipulation of soul energy. They indicate the political character and destiny of nations and show us the origin, function and future of individual races and of the race of mankind as a whole. They indicate the geographic areas of harmony and those of chaos on the surface of our globe and point to future cataclysms and planetary illnesses. They categorize and analyse the reasons for human desire and how these desires may be handled. They give a wider view of karma and offer information as to the mechanics of reincarnation. They can indicate to the earnest student who is prepared to sieve and to meditate, to cross-check and to synthesize, our individual places on the Path.

The full teachings on the Rays expounds the three great laws of Synthesis, Attraction, and Economy, which embrace all other laws of being. For the first time, the nature of fire is explained and categorized under three headings of Electric Fire, Solar Fire and Fire by Friction. It gives intimate knowledge as to the working of hierarchical ashrams and how Masters may be contacted.

The Ray psychology is a sharpened and polished instrument of the sprawling and unwieldy Wisdom of the Ages, and although the psychology must remain esoteric for another hundred years, it is of profound importance to 'the few' who endeavour consciously to reduce the tedium of endless incarnation on the wheel of rebirth. The teaching follows sequentially upon *The Secret Doctrine*, which was a teaching by inference. This, the psychology of the Rays, is a teaching by direct statement. It is the science of the antakarana, the building of the rainbow bridge from personality to Soul.

For the Few Who are Many

In *The Secret Doctrine*, Mme Blavatsky tells us that we are given, in our lives, opportunities to acquire enough of the *right* sort of information to take us to perfection but we have not, within ourselves, the power to synthesize the knowledge we gain. This is indeed true. There is no lack of teachings. Our library shelves are stacked with books and other Halls of Learning are crammed with enough knowledge to make Masters of us all. But that wisdom, the deposit of the Ages, given out by Masters, initiates and disciples, lies practically ignored.

Very few, only a handful in each country, are prepared to take the secret Path to self-mastery. Only the Few will search deeper than the narrow margin of investigation which merely brings comfort to some thwarted aspect of the personality. We search only long enough or deeply enough to find some balm for the wounds we have received from the slings and arrows of outrageous fortune, or for the pangs of despised love. Too many use the occult as a sop for frustration at a personality level. But there are some who do not lose themselves in the savannah of personality which surrounds the deep forest of all-wisdom. There are some who tread so deeply into the unknown, into the occult, that they no longer look for comfort; and, indeed, could not turn back if they wished. For them, there is only the Path and their personality interests become submerged in the more poignant anguish of treading an ever-steepening and narrowing pathway to the summit of the mountain of initiation. To the likes of these, *the few*, are given the powers of synthesis and for *them* was written *The Secret Doctrine*, was fashioned the psychology of the Seven Rays.

The Rays in Man

It is here assumed that the reader has some knowledge of the make-up of man. It is taken for granted that he knows man to possess an upper and lower triad of vehicles through which he is able to express himself; the soul through the upper triad which is, in truth, hardly yet formed in average man; the personality through the lower triad. The two are linked by the antakarana, which in average man is mainly constructed of higher mental substance.

Key to diagram opposite

S	= Soul's vehicle, the upper triad of atma-buddhi-manas.
A	= The Antakarana ... bridge between upper and lower triads, at first made mainly from manasic substance.
P	= The Personality vehicle, made up of the lower mental, emotional and physical bodies.
LM	= Lower mental body, from which is built the Antakarana to the higher triad.
E	= Emotional or Astral body.
Ph	= Gross physical body.

In man's present stage of evolutionary development, *five* Rays mould, manipulate and energize him. Each has a special province of activity, but there is an overlapping. There is a Ray for man's soul. It is not yet possible to distinguish one each for the vehicles of atma-buddhi-manas but merely an overall Ray of the soul and its vehicles or upper triad.

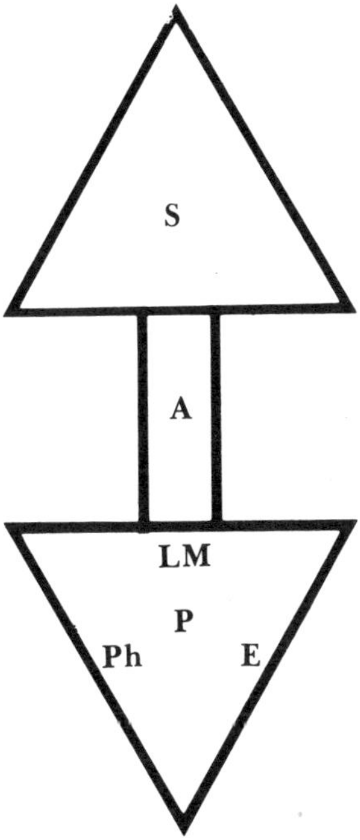

THE SOUL AND ITS VEHICLES

There is a Ray ruling man's gross physical body. There is one ruling his emotional body (or astral, depending on whether we are talking of waking emotions or the active emotional body of sleep). The lower mental body (LM) has a Ray dominating it. The personality vehicle is a real one and comprises a synthesis of the three bodies just mentioned. It sounds its own note, and its integration marks a point of spiritual development and heralds the Third Initiation. It has a Ray of its own. There are thus *five* Rays pouring through man. Animals have only three dominating Rays; and plants, two. In the stage of its present development, only one Ray dominates each element of the mineral kingdom.

For a matter of convenience, in order to express the Ray equipment of an individual, we give a Roman numeral to the Ray of the Soul and assign arabic numbers to the balance. The Rays of the lower triad are bracketed together under the number of the Ray of the personality:-

		5
II	1	6
		3

The Ray Equipment of Dr Baker

A BRIEF ANALYSIS OF THE SEVEN RAYS AND THEIR EXPRESSION IN THE HUMAN KINGDOM

First Ray: Will and Power

Special Virtues:
Strength, courage, steadfastness, truthfulness arising from absolute fearlessness, power of ruling, capacity to grasp great questions in a large-minded way, and of handling men and measures.

Vices of the Ray:
Pride, ambition, wilfulness, hardness, arrogance, desire to control others, obstinacy, anger.

Virtues to be Acquired:
Tenderness, humility, sympathy, tolerance, patience.

Second Ray Love-Wisdom

Special Virtues:
Calm, strength, patience and endurance, love of truth, faithfulness, intuition, clear intelligence, and serene temper.

Vices of the Ray:
Over-absorption in study, coldness, indifference to others, contempt of mental limitation in others.

Virtues to be Acquired:
Love, compassion, unselfishness, energy.

Third Ray: Active Intelligence (Higher Mind)

Special Virtues:
Wide views on all abstract questions, sincerity of purpose, clear intellect, capacity for concentration on philosophic studies,

patience, caution, absence of the tendency to worry himself or others over trifles.

Vices of the Ray:
Intellectual pride, coldness, isolation, inaccuracy in details, absent-mindedness, obstinacy, selfishness, over-much criticism of others.

Virtues to be Acquired:
Sympathy, tolerance, devotion, accuracy, energy and commonsense.

Fourth Ray: Harmony through Conflict

Special Virtues:
Strong affections, sympathy, physical courage, generosity, devotion, quickness of intellect and perception.

Vices of the Ray:
Self-centredness, worrying, inaccruacy, lack of moral courage, strong passions, indolence, extravagance.

Virtues to be Acquired:
Serenity, confidence, self-control, purity, unselfishness, accuracy, mental and moral balance.

Fifth Ray: Concrete Knowledge & Analytical Science (Lower Mind)

Special Virtues:
Strictly accurate statements, justice (without mercy), perseverance, common-sense, uprightness, independence, keen intellect.

Vices of the Ray:
Harsh criticism, narrowness, arrogance, unforgiving temper, lack of sympathy and reverence, prejudice.

Virtues to be Acquired:
Reverence, devotion, sympathy, love and open-mindedness.

Sixth Ray: Devotion & Idealism

Special Virtues:
Devotion, single-mindedness, love, tenderness, intuition, loyalty, reverence.

Vices of the Ray:
Selfish and jealous love, over-leaning on others, partiality, self-deception, sectarianism, superstition, prejudice, over-rapid conclusions, fiery anger.

Virtues to be Acquired:
Strength, self-sacrifice, purity, truth, tolerance, serenity, balance, and commonsense.

Seventh Ray: Ceremonial, Order, Ritual & Magic

Special Virtues:
Strength, perseverance, courage, courtesy, extreme care in details, self-reliance.

Vices of the Ray:
Formalism, bigotry, pride, narrowness, superficial judgements, self-opinion is over-indulged.

Virtues to be Acquired:
Realization of Unity, wide-mindedness, tolerance, humility, gentleness and love.

It should be noted that the above is only a brief analysis of Ray characteristics and can only be applied in a general way. There is much repetition and overlapping because, as previously shown, Rays Four to Six are derived from the three major Rays I, II and III. Most of the characteristics mentioned are of a mental and emotional nature and yet, when describing the purely physical body of a man and its Ray character, it is surprising how these qualities demonstrate in purely physical tissue.

Quite independently of the esoteric psychology, there have been surveys made of the human anatomical types by science and correlations to personality traits have been established. Thus, a *pyknic type* of physical body has been established with broad head, thick shoulders, large chest, and stocky body. They are often happy, carefree persons whose emotional reactions are obvious. They are interested in others apart from themselves. They are extravert. Another type was said to be asthenic, or debilitated.

Through the most careful research over a period of ten years, the writer has found the work of Dr W.H. Sheldon, formerly of Harvard University, to come closest to the Ray approach especially with regard to characteristics of the physical body.

In 1942 Sheldon published his psychology of constitutional differences based on anatomical surveys of thousands of human physiques. (*The Varieties of Temperament* by Sheldon and Stevens.) He distinguished *three* main types, each with seven degrees of intensity. The first type he called the 'ectomorphs' in which there was a preponderance of skin and nervous tissue. They were tall and slender and tended to produce what he called 'cerbrotonic characteristics' of personality. These come closest to what the esotericist would call the *First Ray* type. His second grouping by anatomical analysis was the type with pronounced accent on muscle and bone. They are well built and tend to be the more athletic. He called these 'mesomorphs' and they display somatotonic characteristics of personality. This may be correlated to the *Second Ray* type. Sheldon's third type was the 'endomorph' with accentuation of viscera or intestinal mass. They were plump. stocky and extravert. Some of the personality behaviour patterns of the three types are given below.

Cerebrotonia (Ray I)	Somatotonia (Ray II)	Visceratonia (Ray III)
Restraint in posture and movement, tightness.	Assertiveness of posture and movement.	Relaxation in posture and movement.
Physiological over-response.	Love of physical comfort.	Love of physical adventure.
Over-fast reactions. Love of privacy.	Love of risk and chance.	Love of eating, pleasure in digestion.

Ray I	Ray II	Ray III
Mental over-activity & apprehensiveness.	Bold directness of manner.	Love of polite ceremony.
Secretiveness of feeling.	Spartan indifference to pain.	Sociophilia.
Emotional restraint.	Need of action when troubled.	Greed for affection and approval.
Orientation to old age.	Orientation towards goals and activities.	Orientation to people.
Self-conscious motility of eyes and face.	Over-maturity of appearance.	Easy communication.
Agoraphobia, vocal restraint.	Preference for groups.	Needs people when in trouble.
Poor sleep habits & chronic fatigue.	Claustrophobia.	Orientated towards childhood and family.
Poor routinizing.	Orientated towards his youth.	

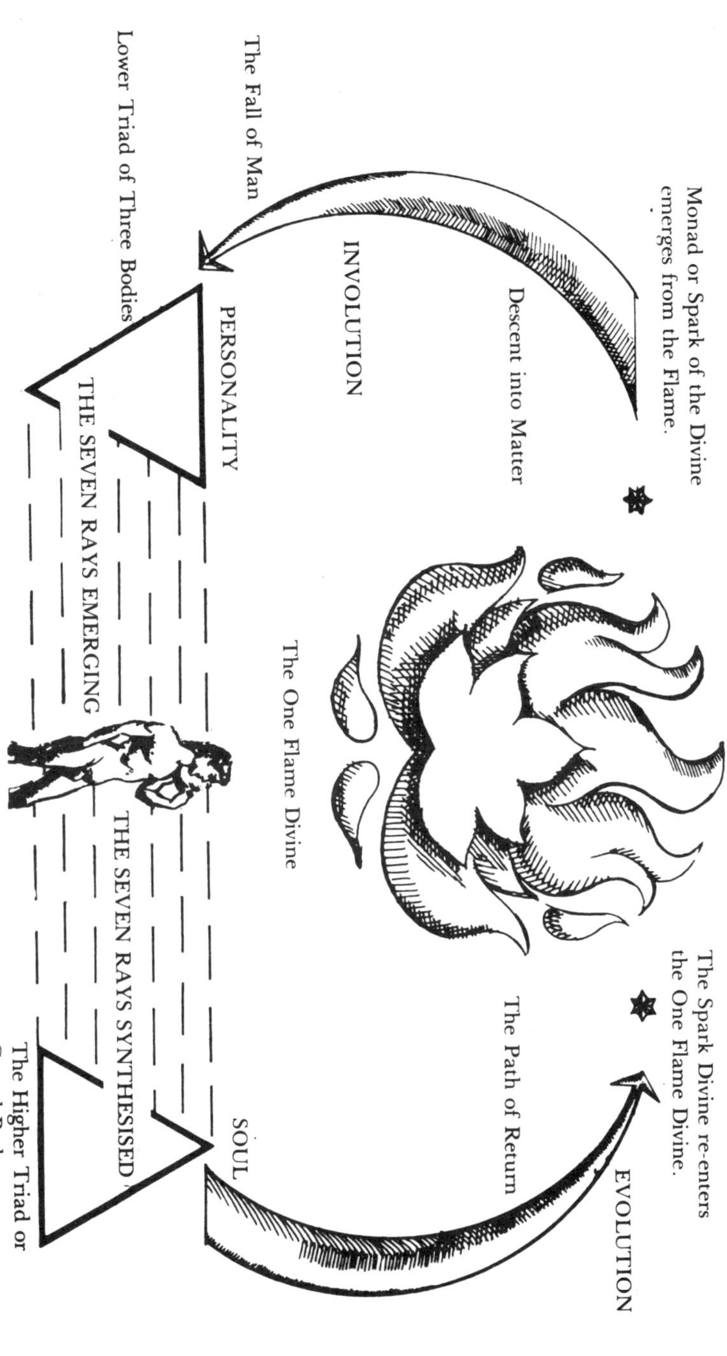

The Spiritual Path of Man Assisted by the Rays

3

In the Beginning ...

The following passage is from *Your Purpose On Earth* by Gemini.

> Long ago ... in the Beginning ... a part of the great Power of Nature (which has been called by many names such as 'God', 'Creator', 'Supreme Being', etc.) was split into billions of Sparks. Each of these Sparks was individual, separated, yet forever connected with Nature by means of an invisible 'wire', because they were still part of that great Power.
>
> ONE OF THESE SPARKS WAS *YOUR* SPIRIT – which is permanent and indestructible.
>
> The sparks existed thus in this state of separation for millions of years and in perfect harmony with Nature. But this happy state of affairs did not continue indefinitely because the time came when you were required to begin building up a law of Earthly experience. The Earth was therefore created and millions of years later the first physical bodies, which were the 'houses' of the individual Sparks (or Spirits) during their Earthly life.
>
> These physical bodies (which, by the way, looked very different from the bodies we have today) were, of course, controlled by the Law of Nature – that Law which governs everything.

The bodies which we, the sparks, occupy one after the other in a great process called reincarnation, are really triple in nature. The triplicity comprises our dense physical body which every man can see for himself and two other subtler bodies which until recently have only been perceived by clairvoyant means. Today, however, thanks to recent developments in scientific equipment, it is possible to distinguish the subtle matter of a mental and emotional body underlying the physical. (See *The Human Aura* by Dr Kilner.)

Into this triad of our bodily equipment, the divine spark enters. Just as a three-sided prism of glass will split white light into seven colours, so too is the Spark divine refracted into seven Rays or divine qualities which permeate colour and direct the activities of the lower triad of the three bodies. These Ray qualities well up within the core of our being and find their way throughout the physical body by means of the *chakras* or energy centres and by subtle paths known as *nadis*.

In each life on earth we are provided with a different triad of bodily equipment into which the seven Rays and their 49 minor or sub-Rays pour in ever-altering combinations. In each life, therefore, the overall colouring or aura varies with an ever increasing tendency to develop a colouring of the three major Rays, which are Red, Indigo and Green, or Rays I, II, III.

This permeation of our vehicles by the all-pervading and quality-bearing Rays of the divine is not peculiar to the human kingdom. The process occurs in the microcosm and in the macrocosm too. Thus, atom, cell, man, and even that great living entitiy which we call the Solar System are flooded and directed by the *Seven Rays*.

When we look at the light of the sun through a prism, we see the Seven Rays which colour the aura of the Solar Logos, of that great entity which uses the threefold body of the sun as a vehicle of incarnation. Were we clairvoyant we could see our own auras too. The spectrum or aura of the sun is seen in two dimensions but the clairvoyant perceives an aura in four dimensions.

Not only do the Seven Rays of our inner being pour out from within us but we are bathed also and continuously by the Seven Rays of the aura of the Solar System in which we live and move and have our being. So really our bodies or lower triads are like battle-grounds in which opposing Rays from within and from without interact. There is a constant changing and mixing of colours and all this reflects in our consciousness, our health and our position on the path. Over many lives our Rays slowly change and there is a sort of repolarization, influenced by continuous rebirth. The purpose of incarnation in matter is to learn to dominate the material world and to add this quality of dominating matter to the Spark within us.

One might well ask 'If the Spark of the Divine is already perfect, how can we add further qualities to it?' Two Grecian urns may be perfect and yet one may have a design added to it. Both remain urns; both remain perfect; and yet the one has had a quality added to it. This may help to explain crudely the metaphysics involved in the problem of the perfect.

But we are concerned here with the Seven Rays and their meaning. As the triad of the three lower bodies undergoes the welter of experience in matter, the three become slowly repolarized over many lives and the symbolically inverted triangle is slowly replaced or rather superimposed by the upright triangle of the soul or causal body.

The Inner Call

This occurs when man begins to release himself from the bonds of the material world and, hearing the inner call of the monad or Spark, starts the longer journey back to his Father's home. Under the processing of the Seven Rays, the consciousness pervading the physical body is shifted to its higher counterpart, the Atmic body. The pervading consciousness of the astral body is transferred to the Buddhic body and in the same way the lower mental body is replaced in function by the Higher Mental body. The channel between the lower and higher mental bodies is the pathway or antakarana through which these major transfers of consciousness are achieved.

After the sixth initiation (or extension of consciousness), the disciple, now a Chohan, no longer uses a physical body but may fashion and use another if the necessity arises. Though all this may seem to involve many abstract principles (and this is true) the process is one of altering vibrations in order to align oneself with the Ray forces or colours.

Thus the Spark of divine white light, originally a son of the Father, or pure flame, enters the world of matter and uses a material form to cognize, comprehend and conquer the material world. Victorious, he turns and faces Calvary and treads the long Path back to the Father.

In the analogy of Light (which is more than an analogy), white light diffuses into only seven in the lower triad or prism; it then returns to its previous purity through the higher prism and is accepted back, a prodigal son, into the Father's home, enriched by his earthly experiences. Had we sufficient awareness we should know that the process is purely one of vibration from start to finish.

The Law of Vibration is the key to measure. It governs the transmutation of differentiated colours back to their synthesis. It controls the breaking up of the One into the seven, and then reabsorption back into the One. It is really the basic law of evolution which necessitates involution.

About 63,000 million monads or Sparks are using the earth chain at the moment to evolve under the Plan. Many of these have used the moon chain as a stepping stone to the life on this planet. On this basis there are twenty monads out of incarnation for each one holding a physical vehicle at this time.

A pebble thrown into Lake Victoria is potentially capable of setting up vibrations in the water which would be felt on the shores of the lake, had we instruments to measure them. So, too, in our Solar System are there vibrations classed under the heading of the Seven Rays which are felt in every part of the Solar Ring-Pass-Not. The great planet Saturn picks Third Ray vibrations because it is predominantly Third Ray in nature. It adds its own vibrations to these and transmits its Third Ray emanations to all entities within the solar system which are Third Ray. In our own bodies the thyroid gland is most susceptible to the Third Ray. It reacts, therefore, strongly to Saturnine influence. The overall result of the latter would be increase in the body's rate of activity as, of course, the Third Ray is the Ray of Active Intelligence.

Every part of the human body reacts more strongly to a certain Ray than to others. From the ancient science of Astrology we are able to ascertain that the spectrum or aura of the sun is correlated by its colours to the parts of the human body. Thus it is found that the colour red and also white light reacts most strongly upon glands and nervous tissue of the head region.

The shape and function of the human body is dependent to a large measure upon the structure of the original chromosomes. The Solar System has been spoken of by Mme Blavatsky and others as a giant cell. A close correspondence exists between the planets and chromosomes. Both carry the forces which mould and assist the developing system of which they are a part. In this last analogy there is contained much food for thought.

Ray Correspondences

When the great planetary bodies of our Solar System, snowballing as comets from their partent body, the sun – except for Neptune which, as H.P.B. says, 'does not belong to our Solar System' – crystallized into coherent centres, they held within them certain great elements derived from their parent sun. These elements can be classified into seven groups, other than the groupings of exoteric science's Periodic Table (arrangement of chemical elements in order of atomic weight).

Our own physical bodies are made of the same elements and we are therefore derived from the sun itself. Our bodily particles are replaced continuously, the process going on all day long. Though this has been long known esoterically, science is only recently possessed of the knowledge that even the fat particles of adipose tissue and the amino acid molecules of proteins are being replaced continuously. We can be quite sure that in the esoterically stated period of seven years, even the skin, teeth and hair are completely replaced. In fact, that physical form that we have so dearly loved in our lives will certainly not be with us in seven years' time. We will possess a completely new physical vehicle which will have been poured into the etheric matrix which we all possess but which changes, too, as it is continually modified by the ever evolving astral, mental and higher bodies which underlie the etheric and physical.

Herein lies the reason for the importance of physical and higher bodily disciplines. Few, very few, people practise these disciplines though they know they ought to, if they partake of occult activity. We are given, at birth, bodies which are of a certain degree of subtlety. It is not usually until after adolescence that we start to corrupt them with smoking and sexual activity, etc., so that it is possible, due to the replacement laws already stated, to provide ourselves as we course through life with bodies less adequate for the work we chose them to perform while in our soul state, than what we had at birth, in fact.

Originally, in the parent sun every atom which we now possess responded to the Seven Great Cosmic Rays pouring into the Solar Body at that time. Now that they are somewhat freed from the sun to undergo evolution in their separate planetary systems, they are not in any way less influenced by the Cosmic Rays still pouring into our Solar System. Some planets, by virtue of their inherent preponderance of one of the seven classes of elements, throw off or reflect as it were more of the corresponding cosmic ray of the preponderant element-class than others. From this esoteric knowledge and the laws which make it up we derive esoteric astrology, from which the present day bastard-type of astrology, in fact exoteric astrology, exists as an offshoot.

As our planets take up an unending, everchanging but easily plotted pattern of positions to that according to the angles that they subtend, and to the directions of planetary bodies from each other, so will their emanations alter in potency and quality; and these influences are picked up and irradiated by every element on this planet earth, including those within our own bodies.

It has been remarked that the planets thus became symbols of a continually recurring septenary which stamps itself on the face of nature and is particularly noticeable in that microcosm which we call man. The persistent repetition of the seven cannot but appear significant to even the superfically minded. It has been known through the ages as the most sacred of numbers and occurs more frequently in scriptural writings than any other number.

Septenary Groups

Mme Blavatsky bears witness to this great Law of Correspondences, invloving seven, in the veiled language of *The Secret Doctrine*. She wrote: 'Remember that physiology, imperfect as it is, shows septenary groups all over the exterior and interior of the body; the seven orifices, the seven "organs" as the base of the brain, the seven plexuses of nerves, etc...' She might also have mentioned as septenaries the seven layers of the epidermis, the seven ductless glands of first importance, the seven methods by which the body is vitalized, the seven major bodily systems, the seven layers of the auric egg, the seven major divisions of the embryo and its tissues, the seven senses (two not yet awakened) and the seven-year periods into which life is divided. Each of these corresponds to a colour, a musical note, a planetary vibration, and a mystical dimension.

In one of his numerous works Paracelsus (1493-1541) remarked:

> The same element that produced Mars, Venus or Jupiter in the sky, exists also in the body of man, because the latter is the son of the astral body of the Macrocosm in the same sense as the physical body of man is the son of the Earth.

Thirty years after *The Secret Doctrine*, the Tibetan devoted a whole treatise in the same Law of Correspondences in that monumental work, *The Treatise on the Seven Rays*.

As the soil is to the sprouting plants, so is the blood related to the living cells of man. Infertility or lack of organic and inorganic nutrition will result in stunted growth or malnutrition and warped activities of the plants. So also with the cells of the human body when the blood is deficient. What the rain is to the soil and the seasons to the sap, so are the emotional and mental emanations of man to the cells of his body, working as they do through the medium of his blood plasma. In a greater way the sun and planets pour out their emanations into the solar cells which we call man. Each man is, indeed, part of the body of a greater being which is the planet we live in.

As Paracelsus said, commenting on the occult significance of the blood: 'The human blood contains an airy, fiery spirit, and this spirit has its centre in the heart, when it is most condensed and from which it radiates, and the radiating rays return to the heart.' He likened the sun to a central heart pumping light, heat and magnetism to every part of the Solar System. 'Our world has its fiery spirit pervading the atmosphere, and its centre is called the Sun, and the influences radiating from the Sun return to that centre.'

Imbalance of Bodily Organs

Occult teachings indicate that when bodily organs go into imbalance, it is more often than not the result of forces aroused in that organ by the corresponding planet on the same Ray as the organ, and its component elements. Paracelsus directed that if a man is deficient in the element whose essence radiates from Mars and consequently suffers from poverty of the blood, he should be given iron. 'If a man gets angry, it is not because he has too much bile, but because the Mars correlative element in his body is in a state of exaltation.'

Again, Kepler (1571-1630), who postulated some great Laws of Physics for the world which in many instances still hold good, practised astrology assiduously and cast the horoscopes of many of the crowned heads of Europe. He said: 'Man is made from the elements, and absorbs them as much as food or drink, from which it follows that man must also, like the elements, be subjected to the influence of the planets.' It is from all this that there has grown up among the esotericists a healing therapy linked to astrology.

The key to the Law of Correspondences is given out in *The Treatise of the Seven Rays*, and through its study we can derive valuable material to form an occult psychology which will assist men across the hurdles of the new Aquarian Age that is upon us.

The great cosmic forces pouring into our Solar System are redirected and intermingled through the action of the Signs of the Zodiac which spread-eagle the heavens about the Solar System. Amongst other things these great constellations may be linked with some accuracy through the Law of Correspondences we have discovered which link up the elements, sounds, colours, foods, tissues, planets, facial features, personality traits, bodies, planes, diseases, etc., thereby attempting a great synthesis which will help us to know ourselves and our fellowmen in true Aquarian style instead of merely accepting them on faith or sufference, characteristic of the dying Age of Pisces.

Let us consider the salt known as iron phosphate, which is associated with the constellation of Pisces. This constellation is humid, lymphatic, plastic, torpid and cold-blooded. The sign often affects the lungs, producing phlegm and mucus. It is a watery sign. The blood itself is 90 per cent water and the endocrine glands, messenger-senders through the hormones, use the watery blood for their purpose. The important oxygen-carrying pigment of the blood is a porphyrin known as haemoglobin, which contains iron in great quantities. Of nearly 5g of iron contained in the body, 70 per cent or more is contained in the blood itself. Iron and its pigment give the blood the ability to carry 60 times more oxygen than if there were no pigment iron compound at all. In fact, if we had water instead of blood we should have to increase our body weight four times to carry sufficient water from which to oxygenate all the cells in the body. Iron phosphate therefore assists the blood's transport system. On a greater scale in the body of the planet it is iron in rolling stock, ships, cars, etc., which plays such an important part in world-transport systems.

Says Dr W.G. Cary in *Chemistry Wonders Of The Human Body*: 'These mighty workers, iron and oxygen, cause all the blood in the body to pass through the heart every three minutes ... health depends on a proper amount of iron phosphate in the blood. When the oxygen carriers are deficient, the circulation is increased in order to conduct a sufficient amount of oxygen to the extremities of the body ... with a diminished quantity of iron on the one hand the motion of the blood must increase, just as seven men must work faster to do the work of ten. This increased motion of blood causes friction, the result of which is heat.'

The heat shows in the body as inflammation and fever. Thus the malfunction of Piscean iron phosphate in the body may cause great bodily stress. It is of help in all cases of inflammation, congestion and haemorrhages, headaches, insomnia, emotional disturbance, feverish colds, anaemia, depression and listless states.

There are two prominent Rays manifesting through Pisces. They are the Second Ray of Love-Wisdom and the Sixth Ray of Devotion and Idealism. These two Rays are close to each other in affinity, the Second Ray ultimately synthesizing the Sixth. The thymus gland and the etheric Heart Centre are aspects of the Second Ray and the planet most concerned with it for men on the Path is Neptune.

The pancreas is the Sixth Ray endocrine gland and the Solar Plexus is the etheric centre. Therefore, when considering the physical body, the planet concerned with the Sixth Ray is Mars. So in this Ray-duality of Pisces we have a leaning on the one hand towards the oxygenating influence of the airy circulation of Aquarius, which lies adjacent to the Second Ray aspect of Pisces — that aspect which concerns the Heart Centre. On the other side of Pisces lies Aries (First and Seventh Rays) ruled by high-powered emotional Mars, and the Sixth Ray aspect of Pisces is drawn to Mars and the Solar Plexus centre. The gland concerned with the Solar Plexus is, as already mentioned, the pancreas. Embryologically related to it, and also on the Sixth Ray, are the liver and gall bladder. The liver is a great storer of iron and is also the powerhouse of the body, its usual temperature being some degrees higher than the rest of the body. It shares a common duct with the pancreas and gall bladder. Virgo is also partly Sixth Ray and lies opposite to Pisces. Too much iron in the iron phosphate of Pisces causes a toxic action in the liver cells. Thus heavy concentration of force in Pisces may well affect the health of the liver in the opposite sign of Virgo. Careful reflection on some of the above correspondences will reveal much to the earnest student of occult physiology and biochemistry.

An afflicted Neptune, ruler of Pisces, may give alcoholic tendencies, acting on the liver thereby through Pisces and its opposition to Virgo.

The Twelve Salts and Associated Signs

Aries: *potassium phosphate*
Taurus: *sodium sulphate*
Gemini: *potassium sulphate*
Cancer: *calcium*
Leo: *silica*
Virgo: *sodium phosphate*
Libra: *calcium fluoride*
Scorpio: *potassium chloride*
Sagittarius: *magnesium phosphate*
Capricorn: *calcium phosphate*
Aquarius: *sodium chloride*
Pisces: *iron phosphate*

4

Seven Ray Qualities

Seven Ray qualities suggested by keywords:

Ray I: *power*
Ray II: *love-wisdom*
Ray III: *abstract mind*
Ray IV: *harmony through conflict*
Ray V: *concrete mind*
Ray VI: *devotion*
Ray VII: *ceremonial order, activity or organization*

It is helpful to synthesize one's Ray thinking in such a manner that a certain homogeneity is seen and their unity in Ray-relationship becomes clearer. Remembering constantly that 'all is energy' at different levels of manifestation, the Seven Rays may be seen in two main divisions, or streams of that energy.

The Two Streams

Rays I, III, V, and VII are concerned with what has been called the form side of manifestation; while Rays II, IV, and VI are expressive of the life side. Thus Power or Will, Mind and Organization form, as it were, the channel or vessel for Love, Beauty (or Harmony) and Devotion.

Another view one may take is to see Rays I and VII, II and VI, and III and V, as three sets of pairs or dualities in which the second one of the pair reflects the first at a more material level.

Ray I of Power is reflected in the organizing qualities of Ray VII; Ray II of Love-Wisdom will work out in personality levels as devotion, while the Abstract Mind principles of Ray III filter into the human brain as lower or Concrete thoughts embodied in Ray V.

The Ray of Humanity

All the Rays are equally important to us but at this time, some are more actively moulding civilization than others. To begin with, Ray IV is of great import being the special Ray of humanity as a whole, so that Harmony through Conflict is more obviously our mode of achievement at this time. It also accentuates the numerical value of the number four since we are in the Fourth Round of the Fourth Great Chain, and Atlantis peopled the Fourth Root Race (of this Fourth Round).

Four is the halfway mark between Seven, and we may note with encouragement that after the halfway period of the Atlantean Root Race (the Fourth), we are past the densest periods of the Chain, Round and Root Races, for humanity is well into the Fifth or Aryan Root Race and there are still two more Root Races to come.

Ray Five

But to return to the Rays in the light of the latter remarks, our membership of the Fifth (or Aryan) Race during which we have developed the lower mind (almost over-developed it) shows the influence and importance of Ray V at this time. The atomic discoveries and continued research in that direction have so far marked the highest achievements of the brain-mind.

But fortunately for this planet there is always the overall Ray of the Solar System which is persistently active, and we may well pray that its exalting and ennobling influences will continue to guide the fine Fifth Ray activities in the direction of true evolution.

The New Age

The fact that Ray VI, which rules the Piscean era, is on the way out and that of Ray VII (ruling the Aquarian Age) is approaching, and that we are now in the transition period between the two conflicting influences is well known to many in the world today. The spreading of the knowledge regarding this change-over, backed by factual astronomical data and by astrological teaching concerning the sun's entry into a new constellation of the zodiac is something that might well dispel the despondency of those about us who see bewildering changes and immense conflict everywhere.

Assessing the Rays

While it is not so very easy at our level of development to assess either our own Rays or the Rays of others with any great degree of accuracy, we can nevertheless study the whole Ray philosophy and through it apply what we can to the understanding of our fellow men. This most revealing 'Spiritual Psychology of the Future' is of tremendous importance in assessing the character of men, their behaviour and also the nature of the group or nation to which they belong.

In this matter we should consider, too, the level on the evolutionary ladder of those we are assessing. There are old souls and young souls, soul-age being gauged not by physical years but by the number of incarnations a soul has experienced in the many different and succeeding personalities. Ray quality and soul age determine the amazing complexity of the human unit.

Soul Age

With regard to soul age, the Tibetan has stated that it is the existence of a deep sense of responsibility that marks the true disciple. This does not, however, imply any niggling fussiness nor the minding of someone else's business! The question 'How much do I or does he or she really *care at heart* about humanity?' should bring some realization as to the age of the soul.

Misuse of the Rays

There is a method which might appear to be on the negative side for clearing the ground towards Ray assessment. Through detecting the lower aspects of Rays, the so-called 'vices' which an excess of a Ray quality may lead on to, we come to an understanding of how that vice manifests on a higher level.

The Ray Characteristics

For example, love of power, excessive emotion and self-dramatization can indicate, respectively, uncontrolled First, Sixth and Fourth/Seventh Ray qualities. (The last mentioned revel sometimes in outer trappings and display!) Knowledge of such excess or misuse of a Ray quality will indicate the very 'route', line or channel for change or transmutation into the self-same quality on a higher level of its own expression.

Further Information

The Seven Rays, the sevenfold energy of God, constitute the basis of all that *is*. In the Christian Scriptures they are symbolically described as the Seven Spirits Before The Throne. Their mighty power is stepped down and modified as they enter our Solar System through the Twelve Gates (of Revelations), which are really the twelve signs of the Zodiac. They express within all that exists the seven fundamental qualities of which everything from atom to highest Spiritual Intelligence is composed.

Rays I, II, and III, called the Rays of Aspect, underlie the Trinitarian teachings of the World Religions. From the last of these three great primaries, the Third Ray, there streams the other four Rays known as the Rays of Attribute. These categorical statements are required as a minimum basis for understanding that which follows and are not meant to be accepted without questioning, study and contemplation, to which at all times it is hoped the reader will resort.

Of what value is it to study and assimilate knowledge of the Seven Rays? Since they comprise the all-embracing, life-side of the Ageless Wisdom's philosophy, such study throws light on the nature of the seeker's own life, his special qualities, as well as his specific value to the whole scheme of creation, insignificant though he may be from one aspect. It links him in an understanding, life-relationship with a person or problem, be that problem individual, national or world-wide. Situations are being increasingly approached from the standpoint of their meaning or, deeper still, from the level of causes rather than from the level of effects only. The effects themselves become more fully understood and in a different spirit.

History sheds its disproportionate aspects and distortions, and the underlying reasons for world events become somewhat clearer when it is realized that evey nation is in special affinity with one or two of the Rays. All seven Rays cycle into and out of manifested power in accordance with certain time cycles which may endure one decade or a thousand decades. In these rhythmic cycles of time we may sense the great rhythms of creation itself, called in Hindu symbolic religious phraseology 'The Dance of Shiva'.

That most important statement, namely, that 'all is energy', a fact now accepted by science, is basic to a study of the Seven Rays and must always be kept in mind when considering the subject, for in this factual statement we have the cause of the underlying unity between the Ageless Wisdom's teaching and the very ancient science of astrology. For the Seven Rays underlie, permeate and condition the planets in their courses, and although our earth is one of the least advanced of the planets within our Solar System, and since all are linked by distinct but invisible bonds, it is nevertheless of great importance to that whole of which it, the earth, forms a part.

These principles of Being – for such they are – are true of each one of us individually, God having made man in His own image. For with our own individual Ray make-up and our unity in the underlying sevenfold energy, we are as important to our planet, and therefore to the Solar System, as each organ of the body and each cell of those organs is important to its own specific whole which in turn forms part of a greater one. Atom, man, planet, solar system, and beyond, are ONE in, and are coloured by, this sevenfold energy stream which is God Himself in manifestation.

There are certain other fundamental statements which must be made and understood gradually by the reader before entering into anything more discursive and in detail.

Spirit, Soul and Personality

Every solar system (and ours is on the Second Ray), every planet and every human being responds to one of these mighty Seven Rays and to any or several of the other six, according to (from the human standpoint) the need of the soul and its work in any one incarnation. Here we need to note the following:-

1. *The Spirit* or Monad of each one of us is always and unchangingly on one of the three Major Rays of either Will, Love-Wisdom or Divine Intelligence.
2. *The Soul* can be on any one of the Rays for many incarnations, changing to one of the three Major Rays during discipleship.
3. *The Personality* as a totality is on one Ray while its three component parts, Mind, Emotions and Physical Body, each respond to a specific Ray. Any one of these can remain the same for more than one incarnation, but usually change from life to life according to the soul's need for experience, or for certain qualities which must be developed.

In every kingdom of nature there is a peak of attainment along each Ray. In the mineral kingdom the peak of attainment is reached in the precious stones. For example, the diamond marks the apotheosis of those units in that kingdom working along the First Ray of will and power. Within the animal kingdom a domestic animal of one type heads each Ray. It is said that the dog is on the Second Ray, the horse on the Sixth, the cat on the

Third and the elephant on the First. The few existing authorities differ interestingly on the subject.

To return to the Fourth kingdom of nature, the human, we find that *as a whole* it is allied to the Fourth Ray of Harmony through Conflict at this stage of its progress. As each human begins to pass out of his kingdom into the super-human kingdom, after the third initiation, he expresses increasingly the Ray of his Monad or Spirit until, at the fifth initiation and beyond, he becomes a perfect exemplar of one of these Seven mighty streams of Cosmic Energy or Rays. He is then ready to tread the way of the Higher Evolution along one of the Seven Paths ... a Way known only to the higher initiates and to those beyond.

This is new study! It stems from the most ancient teachings ever known. It was taught by Mme Blavatsky in *The Secret Doctrine*, scattered (purposely, some think) through its many pages in obscure terminology. Annie Besant and C.W. Leadbeater gave out some further knowledge of the Rays in a simplified form. Later, a much fuller insight into the subject and a considerably more detailed teaching was given on the Rays by the Tibetan teacher writing through Mrs A.A. Bailey. Geoffrey Hodson and Professor Ernest Wood have also contributed significantly to available knowledge. Students are advised to search for themselves in earlier works, though it is more than likely that the 'Bailey Books' will provide the deepest and widest fields of investigation.

5

Planes and Energy Centres

Like the moon we also have our 'dark fortnight', our waning cycle when there is less intelligent intake during occult studies. It is then that we should stop and consider first principles. Then we may begin again with a different mental focus, in greater clarity and with a somewhat deeper understanding of the subject.

Rotating Spheres

The following is taken from *A Treatise On Cosmic Fire*. Therein the Tibetan Master describes three fundamental modes of motion in the universe:

1. Rotary
2. Spiral-Cyclic
3. Forward-Progressive

All three can be seen in connection with the seven Rays, but at present we shall apply the first of these only, namely Rotary Motion.

It is stated that the seven Planes, regarded as seven vast spheres, rotate *latitudinally* within the solar periphery, and that the seven Rays, seven spheroidal bands of 'colour' regarded as the seven veiling forms of 'The Spirits Before the Throne of God' rotate *longitudinally*.

These two sets of spheres, the seven Rays and the seven Planes, together result in a 'vast interlocking network' forming the entire Solar System and producing the latter's own spheroidal shape. Each Plane is a vast sphere of matter actuated by latent heat, progressing or rotating in one particular direction. Each Ray of light, no matter what the colour, is likewise a sphere of matter of the utmost tenuity, rotating at right angles to that of the planes.

The planes rotate from East to West.

The Rays rotate from North to South.

We are not here referring to points in space; we are simply making this distinction and employing words to make an abstruse idea more comprehensible.

The Tapestry of Life

We might see these two great component parts of our Solar System as the warp and woof of an immense tapestry. For design we have the *planets* with their various kingdoms of nature in their different stages of development. Threading in and out in scintillating gold, silver and an irridescence of many colours we have the intricate embroidery, a design of many patterns, shapes and sizes within the framework of our particular Solar System, seven planets constituting one celestial family — of which our earth is a relatively minor member.

Relation of Rays, Planes and Qualities

Here we might consider the relation in quality or 'colouring' between each Ray and Plane; but we should realize that in another solar system, the scale of correspondences would be different due to different stages of evolution and to reasons quite beyond and unknown to our minds.

Ray I of Power is related to the highest plane, called the plane of Adi or Spirit.

Ray II of Love-Wisdom is related to the second plane, Anupadaka, called the Monadic plane. It is the plane of our own Monads and conditions them all because this is a Second Ray solar system, bearing out the oft-quoted saying that 'God is Love'.

Ray III of Divine Mind is correlated with the third plane of Atma or Will, suggesting the quality needed for human mind-control.

Ray IV of Harmony is seen as connected with the fourth plane of Buddhi or Intuition.

Ray V of Mentality is associated with the fifth or Mental plane.

Ray VI of Idealistic Devotion is equated with the sixth plane of Emotion.

Ray VII of Ordered Service (and ceremonial activity) is connected with the physico-etheric plane.

Here, for easy reference, is the tabulation:

RAY and QUALITY			PLANE and QUALITY	
Ray I	Power	1	**Adi**	Pure Spirit
Ray II	Love-Wisdom	2	**Anupadaka**	Monadic
Ray III	Divine Mind	3	**Atma**	Will
Ray IV	Harmony	4	**Buddhi**	Intuition
Ray V	Mentality	5	**Manas**	Mind
Ray VI	Devotion	6	**Astral**	Emotion
Ray VII	Ordered Activity	7	**Physico-etheric**	Physical

Correlation

The Pythagorean System taught the importance of Number, and the correlation between the number of a Ray and the correspondingly numbered plane with the thus shared similarity of quality is a fruitful subject for thought.

Particularly at this time, we should consider the outgoing Sixth Ray of the Piscean era and the incoming Seventh Ray of Aquarius, their qualities being related to the sixth and seventh planes respectively. We should investigate the qualities now fading out and those we can expect to manifest in the future, and remember that always the negative aspects appear first. Is it not true at this time of chaos in the world when the quality of the incoming Seventh Ray is really 'Ordered Activity?'

Our Own Monad and Soul Rays

Having a Ray and Plane tabulation before us indicating the high spiritual level of the human monad, we can readily understand why it takes time for our brains to register which Ray our Monad belongs to. However, it is not quite profitless to speculate, provided one knows that only faint intimations of it are registered in the consciousness and that all monads are (for *our* planetary evolution) only on any one of the first three (major) Rays.

It is less difficult to determine the Ray of one's soul (or ego) since its lowest level of existence is the higher part of the Mental plane. We should in fact try to ascertain this, for such attempts strengthen the soul's control and its connection with the personality. It helps to build the bridge between the higher and lower mind and the fresh focus of vision spoken about at the beginning of this chapter.

To induce the knowledge of our soul's quality and to bring that quality into action, a sustained question broached inwardly and worded somewhat as follows, can be helpful:

> In times of greatest stress or need, do I rely mostly on mind (III), love (II), or power-will (I), to bring about a result or deal with a problem?

Of course we use all three, but in the last analysis one of these is usually the more constant or else the final resort. In time, such an existing 'open question' resting in the mind will indicate whether the soul belongs to one of the three major Rays of Aspect, and to which one; or, as it is quite likely, to one of the Rays of Attribute, namely, IV, V, VI, VII.

Relationship to a Master of the Wisdom

For many lives the soul remains on one of the Rays of Attribute, changing to one of the major three of Aspect during discipleship in its earlier or later stages. Knowledge about some of the Masters and their work in connection with the Rays, and one's own feeling of attraction to some particular line of work of one of the Great Ones, will often give a strong indication of one's soul Ray.

The Energy Centres

(*The Energy Centres are shown in descending order overleaf.*)

Head Centre:

Ray 1: Bright Red: Pineal Gland: Plane of Adi: Zodiacal Signs – Aries and Leo: Seventh Root Race: Fire: Uranus: The Sun: Will and Power.

Ajna Centre:

Ray 5: Orange: Pituitary Gland: Manasic Plane: Zodiacal Sign – Aquarius: Fifth Root Race: Fire: Venus: Science and Concrete Knowledge.

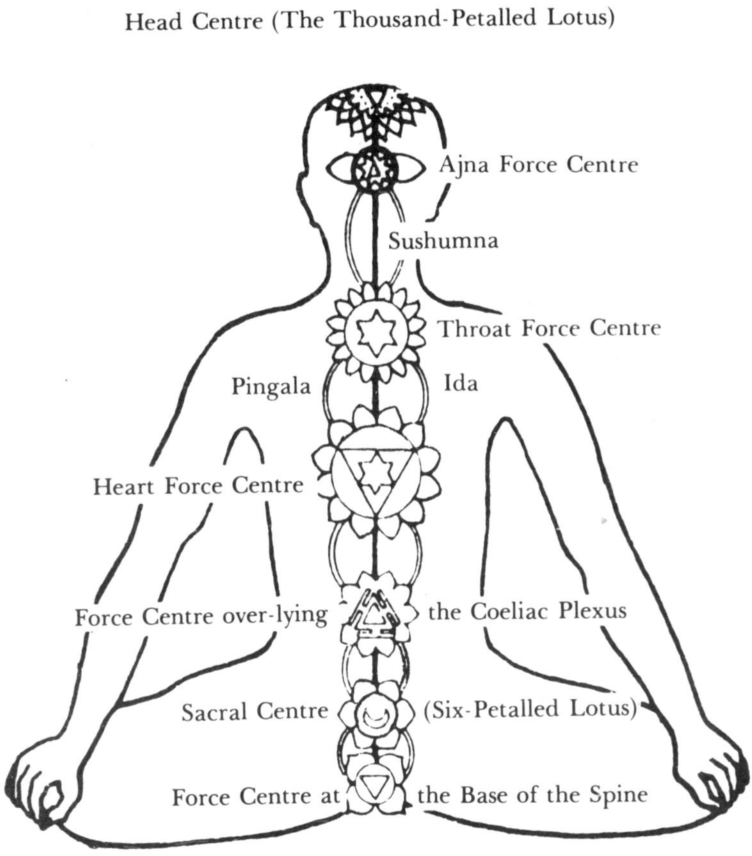

Throat Centre:
Ray 3: Green: Thyroid Gland: Mental Plane: Zodiacal Signs – Capricorn, Cancer, Libra: Fifth Root Race (not on the Path): Air: Saturn: Active Intelligence.

Heart Centre:
Ray 2: Indigo: Orange: Thymus Gland: Logoic Plane: Zodiacal Signs – Gemini, Pisces, Leo: Sixth Root Race: Intuition: Neptune, Jupiter: Love-Wisdom.

Spleen Centre:
Note: *This centre is becoming dormant in advanced man. It does not have an 'alter ego' in the sense that, for instance, the Head Centre is the alter ego of the Centre at the Base of the Spine. Energies taken directly into this centre are transmitted to the Seven minor Head Centres which are closely related to the brain.*

Solar Plexus Centre:
Ray 6: Rose, Blue: Pancreas: Astral Plane: Zodiacal Signs – Virgo, Pisces: Fourth Root Race (not on the Path): Water: Mars, Jupiter: Devotion and Idealism.

Base of the Spine Centre:
Ray 4: Deep Yellow: Suprarenal Glands: Buddhic Plane: Zodiacal Signs – Scorpio, Taurus: Fourth Root Race: Buddhi: Mercury: Art & Harmony through Conflict.

Sacral Centre:
Ray 7: Gonads: Physico-Etheric Plane: Zodiacal Sign – Cancer: Moon, Uranus: Third Root Race: Earth: Ceremonial Order.

Part Two

THE QUALITIES OF LIFE

6

First Ray: Will and Power

The psychology of the Seven Rays is for the very few. It is for the few who, thinly sprinkled across all lands, are many. It is for those who are beginning to suffer from 'divine unrest'. By divine unrest I do not mean those who are in revolt against their mere circumstances, against their dharma, or their karma. Not those who only suffer 'the slings and arrows or outrageous fortune' or who are wincing under their inabilities to achieve their material ambitions.

I speak here for that few, that very few, who in this and other incarnations have known all of life's joys and sorrows, who, in most instances, could, if they choose, be at the top of any of the professions or the arts, and may well be now, but for whom there still exists an urge, in inner, unrequited urge that demands a search in pastures new.

The psychology of the Seven Rays is for those who no longer need to seek in material things for a momentary peace of mind. It is for those who seek the eternal qualities of the soul. It teaches how to accomplish this withdrawal from enmeshment with matter without losing the power, the love and the spirit of sacrifice which we have distilled from all the ferment of our earthly struggles. It makes no call to those who have not yet experienced but to those who *have* and yet still seek something else. It does not call for withdrawal from the very front line of service, in which most of us exist but gives us the wherewithal to stand firmly in one kingdom of life whilst equipping us for a life that also exists, even in the heat of battle in the kingdom within.

'Thou preparest a table before me in the presence of mine enemies ...'

The psychology of the Seven Rays prepares the few for the 'burning ground' which comes when every call of the flesh has been answered and found wanting, when every material mesh has clung and finally fallen from you. It is a process of self-immolation which comes easiest to those richest in experience but poorest in attachment to those same experiences. Because the 'burning ground' is so appropriately First Ray in the concepts that it conjures up in the mind, I might be forgiven for quoting some relevant passages from *The Ravings of a Mystic* which I wrote seven years ago. The article probably marked the end of my 'angry young man' period:

If you have never kown the sickening thrill of a straight-flush, if you have never paused, guilty, 'in the rank sweat of an ensemened bed', or clapped your hands to ears that would shut out the screams of scorching tank-entombed men, or, true blue, have never quelled the nausea of protesting organs with gushes of C_2OH_5, or, friendless in the great alone have never heard the winds speak, or the earth move; or, hounded by some unknown force, have not plunged deep in every glittering pool and have not emerged from all these crying ever, 'Not this! Not this!' then these words are not for you.

The Burning Ground is not for you, not yet; not until every call of the flesh is answered, not until every material mesh has clung to you. But when richest in experience – experience beyond your wildest dreams – and when poorest in attachment to them, then comes the Burning Ground.

Then Paul, three days blinded by the shaft of light; then Hiram Abiff taking the blow; then Arjuna on the field of battle; then St Augustine, reeling before the City of God; then Lulley confronting the cancerous breast; then Socrates drinking the hemlock; then More facing the scaffold; then Swedenborg's madness and Bacon's treason; then all will have meaning. For you, the initiate, there will be the end of your cry of 'Not this!' Instead, from the cliffs of your own mind you will proclaim for all initiates to hear, 'This!' and joyfully you will tread your way back down the mountainside and take up your yoke next to your fellowman, knowing full well why you pull, what you pull, and where to pull it. This comes to everyone.

It comes in that last desperate and bitter 'run-in' of incarnations that pins us in quick succession to the crosses of the Zodiac.

It comes to us after the welter of all our experiences in many lives on earth has brought us to our knees. Armed with the self-reliance and integration of personality, which our broad, varied and intense experiences have brought us, we, the self-reliant, can survive the Burning Ground, 'The lover, the madman and the poet are of imagination compact.' It is the crises survived that matter and not the ecclesiastical or commercial or social rank of the man.

Out of this welter of experience, slowly there emerges the few in every generation. The English Master, Robert Browning, described them thus:

For men begin to pass their nature's bound,
And find new hopes and cares which fast supplant
Their proper joys and griefs; they grow too great
For narrow creeds of right and wrong, which fade
Before the unmeasured thirst for good; while peace
Rises within them ever more and more.
Such men are even now upon the earth,
Serene amid the half-formed creatures round.

The Ray of Will and Power is one facet of seven used for the expression of divinity in man. With the other rays, it constantly forms, maintains and destroys the various bodies of man. In every one of us there is to be found the Ray of Will and Power. In some of our vehicles it is more potently expressed than others. Though basically 'perfect' (because they are divine), the Rays manifest their qualities in man as virtues and vices at a personality level. But they rule all kingdoms and are responsible for the qualities of physical form in mineral, plant and animal as well as in man. The Ray of Will and Power is called the First Ray, although it is only a sub-ray of the great Ray of Love-Wisdom which rules our Solar System.

The Creator, Maintainer and Destroyer

The Ray of Will and Power plays the greatest part in the evolution of form and therefore rules the physical body of man. Most especially, in the human kingdom, its energies are manipulated by the Manus of the races. Each Race and Sub-Race has a Manu, who originally founded the race, strengthened it by actually incarnating in it at points of time and location when and where the race needed strengthening.

The Lord of the Fifth Root Race, our own, is Vaivasvata Manu, whose stock flows in the blood of every one of us. In the earliest days of the Race, known as the Aryan (but not to be confused with the Hitlerian concept), He acted as a sort of Moses, teaching the race the disciplines of body and mind which were to ensure its survival for the great work of unfoldment of planetary consciousness which lay ahead for the Race.

Through men like Lycurgus of Sparta, the First Ray works. Through the efforts of Lycurgus, the Greeks were later to throw off the marauding hordes of Persians who threatened survival of the Grecian and Roman sub-race of the Aryan. His spartan discipline and code has become part of the tradition of the Fifth Race. The Manus, and their elect, carry in their aurae and permanent atoms the racial characteristics which act like the genes and chromosomes in the living cell. (The First Ray rules the nucleus of the cell and the atom wherein lie the organizing and empowering forces of those microcosms).

The Manus plant their characteristics continuously in the Race, where they are mutated and improved upon during the Race's unfolding history. The Manu reabsorbs the newly-won qualities and holds them for later use. Thus, we have the reincarnation of Ancient Rome in the British Commonwealth, a process of development guided by Vaivasvata.

The Lords of Karma work through the First Ray, too. And via the genes and chromosomes they exact their cruellest debts in physical deformity. And so, a fast developing soul, for instance, in life after life, may waste away his talents in incessant and useless activity. The Lords of Karma through the First Ray might intercede, slow down and eliminate this serious defect by imposing a series of lives in a crippled or paralysed form.

The Ray in Politics

The First Ray, as one would have guessed, rules fascism, ultra-conservatism and despotism, whereas the Second Ray of Love-Wisdom rules democracy and the Third Ray, socialism. With Ray One, the accent is upon 'Might is Right'. Hitler was the arch-prince of Fascism. He was the Destroyer aspect rampant, the Machiavelli of the twentieth century. He was said to have had some direct contact with the forces of Shamballa.

Shamballa	Ray I
The Hierarchy	Ray II
Mankind	Ray III

Shamballa is said to be the place 'Where the Will of God is known' and recreates form ever anew by shattering the old and crystallized. It inspires the frontiersman who breaks down old barriers and hews out new paths and then (often unwillingly) stands aside for the Fourth Ray builders of culture and refined taste to entrench their newly-won attributes and to elaborate on them.

There is no better poetic illustration of these First Ray qualities and vices to be found in the English language outside of Dryden's description of the politically-minded First Ray personality of the Earl of Shaftesbury in 'Absalom and Achitophel':-

> A daring pilot in extremity,
> Pleased with the danger, when the waves went high,
> He sought the storms; but, for a calm outfit,
> Would steer to nigh the sands to boast his wit ...
> In friendship false, implacable in hate,
> Resolved to ruin or to rule the state ...
> Sagacious, bold and turbulent of wit,
> Restless, unfixed in principles and place,
> In power unpleased, impatient of disgrace ...

We shall later see how close this description is to a First Ray mind, emotional body or personality.

It is not surprising, therefore, that the religion of Judaism is ruled by the First Ray, as is also the Jewish Race itself. The Ram (Aries) was a most prominent symbol amongst the Jews and figured in their sacrificial rites. Judaism has a most clearly demarcated monotheism. It contains the concept of a wrathful and revengeful God demanding 'an eye for an eye' in true karmic and First Ray style.

Karmic Clearing House

Because of its Ray equipment the Jewish Race has been able to survive against impossible odds. Isolation comes to it easily and in such isolation the culture of the Jew often flourishes. The Jew can show all the necessary one-pointed-ness of the First Ray in both religion and in business. He often dresses loudly and is quick to demonstrate his success with ostentatious living all through the week until Saturday and then vanishes into austerity, isolation and devotion to his ancestral form of worship without any ado. It is no wonder that people with First Ray equipment have an unequalled opportunity to work off karma. The Tibetan says that the Jewish race is a karmic clearing house for souls overloaded with difficult karma. Some of us tend to accumulate an excess of karma through a cycle of lives. We then choose a Jewish body in order to be certain of opportunities to work that karma off.

This ability to isolate and thrive is seen clearly in the First Ray approach to idealism which appears to the observer as both callous and insincere. A First Ray will approach an ideal and give his all to it (never less!). He will drive it with every human (and some say super-human) energy and then, when another ideal comes along that is higher, he will switch over to it without compunction and with a completeness that is devastating to those on the Sixth Ray, devoted to idealism. The First Ray may then even turn on the older ideal and destroy it in order to be free for unstinting energizing of the succeeding ideal.

If he respects someone, he will take orders from that one in true martial style, but, unlike the Sixth Ray, he must be left alone to work out for himself how to implement the commands given him. When they drive an ideal, they will proclaim it from the roof tops. They will unfurl gaudy banners and draw to themselves and their ideals the brazen blare of public attention. And come what odds, they will, even in failure, confound their opponents with their tenacity of purpose, their one-pointed and unrelenting devotion.

To the exasperation of their competitors, they will press on regardless (Aries); they will live on the smell of an oil-rag (Capricorn) and climb the sheer face of the mountain in preference to the longer but easier way. They will stand on a desolate outcrop or lie for years in exile until their time is right. They will win their point or die in the effort.

An understanding of these dominant points of First Ray approach is important because they illustrate the profound difference which is accorded to disciples on the First Ray and those on the Second Ray of Love-Wisdom. The neophyte on the Ray of Love-Wisdom is gently coaxed and constantly kept within the aura of the Master. He is most easily reached by visual and mystical impression. He can draw continuously on the ashram for energy and encouragement. His period of instruction is protracted and his tasks are those of building and integrating, working in groups and most frequently at subjective levels.

Recharging of Subjective Energies

Not so with the disciple on the First Ray. When a task is assigned him, he is given a minimum of instruction, usually accompanied with a vast but brief recharging of his subjective energies. He is then 'on his own', and although he knows that he is helped where possible by his occult superiors, he must fend for himself and take the consequences on his own shoulders for the results of his First Ray techniques, though these techniques are the very ones needed for the task involved ... and the task is usually a difficult one ... perhaps to hold a bridgehead of some important aspect of hierarchical work secure in a hostile world, come what may ... to break down some entrenched and crystallized thought form or organized group, blocking the way of man's progress ... or to create some new form and hold it until the public grows to accept (and therefore to energize) it.

His training is so often harsh, telescoped into short periods of time and accompanied by stress-producing stimulation. He is given seed thoughts or impressions and must search and rack his intuition to obtain the growth of them into meaningful and synthesized organisms. They work alone with their own methods. They give no quarter and expect none. Their training and final infusion with *love* forms a very definite course of development and unfoldment.

Surprisingly, it is self-pity that is the First Ray disciple's greatest weakness and it is out of this condition that some of the worst of the Ray's vices stem.

Vices of the Ray:
Pride, ambition, wilfulness, hardness, arrogance, desire to control others, obstinacy, anger.

Virtues to be Acquired:
Tenderness, humility, sympathy, tolerance, patience.

Special Virtues:
Strength, courage, steadfastness, truthfulness arising from absolute fearlessness, power of ruling, capacity to grasp great questions in a large-minded way, and of handling men and measures.

> Oh Lord, I have been praying day after day unceasingly for months, and you have not answered.
> Young man, I'm only waiting for you to stop shouting!

7
Second Ray: Love-Wisdom

The Second Ray has a particular meaning and special signfificance because it corresponds to the fundamental 'note' of that Great Being which uses our solar system as His visible body of manifestation: the Solar Logos has Love-Wisdom for its basic quality.

These teachings give the profound explanation and the justification for the religious and mystical affirmation: *God is Love*.

The mystics felt and perceived clearly that God in his most universal, transcendent and absolute aspect — Parabrahman — is the *all* and one cannot attribute to him any quality or particular note in preference to the others. God, manifested by our own solar system, that is the Solar Logos, is above all *love*, and the Law of Life is the Law of Love.

But this Divine Love is understood in the highest and purest and most universal sense. It was Love that was the profound motive determining the manifestation, and it is Love that maintains its order and rhythm.

Love guides all Beings along the Path of Return to the Father; Love works for the perfection of all that lives. Love creates the forms which temporarily house Life hidden in it, and the same Love produces disintegration of those forms so that Life can continue onward. Taken as a whole, this Love is then Supreme Wisdom.

The Ray of Love-Wisdom shows itself in reflections from plane to plane and in various beings, always limiting itself to the qualities and imperfections of the various grades of entities of which those planes are made up.

Every Ray has an affinity and connection with a given first plane, the other which corresponds to it numerically. Thus, the First Ray of Will and Power is connected with the First Plane of Manifestation, the Plane of Agni, also known as the 'Sea of Fire'.

The Second Ray, on the other hand, has a particular connection with the Second Plane, the Monadic, but then it also tends to show itself in the planes complimentary to this one. The Fourth or Buddhic, and the Sixth, the Astral or Emotive.

Translating this data into human psychological terms and starting from the bottom, one can say that the Love which shows itself in the world of the emotions corresponds to love of the personality, passionate or sentimental love, pervaded by desire, limited to one or few beings.

This Love, with the progressive evolution of man, is enlarged, purified and elevated as far as the Ego, or Soul, or groups that are even larger until the whole of humanity is involved and included.

Sublime Love of the Monad

Yet this Love can become even higher and even more vast, more universal, to inculde Hierarchies of Beings other than human, achieving a unity with all that lives in the entire solar system and even radiates beyond this so far as to become cosmic. This is the sublime Love of the Monad.

It follows that Love, while in the primitive and more human stages, also has egoistical and separative aspects and can, with its tenacious attachments, passionate intoxications, and sweet enchantments, constitute an obstacle to spiritual development.

It becomes, in its further stages, a potent means of spiritual elevation and expansion, helping to break the narrow incasement of the separated 'I', and transforming desire into aspiration, the thirst to possess into that impetus of dedication, the wish for the individual completion into gradual unification with the Universal Life.

Certainly, such a conquest, this purification and sublimation, is not achieved without acute suffering and harsh toil, even in a life that is directed and in a certain sense, of minor resistance. This is true, above all, for those who, by basic constitution, belong to the Second Ray, while those who belong to other Rays must follow other lives and lines of development.

Though one can say that in a certain sense, the Life of Love and Sublimation is the central life for everyone, because in a world (Solar System) in which Love predominates, we can consider all the other Rays as sub-Rays of the Second Ray. Thus, while many souls belong to other Rays, the vibration of the Second strikes them all and causes them to pulsate.

What now of the other aspect of this two-fold Ray, the aspect of *Wisdom*?

It is highly significant that Love and Wisdom, which seem first and foremost, two qualities that are different and independent, constitute two aspects of the same Ray of Divine Quality.

A deeper examination gives a clear reason for this fact. There cannot really be a spiritual Love, truly beneficial, disinterested and inclusive, unless it is pervaded by Wisdom. Without this, Love can wander and over-reach its limits. On the other hand, Wisdom, isolated from Love, an impersonal vision of Reality, would remain cold and inactive, unless it were pervaded by Love's warm flame.

These two notes – Eros and Logos – bring together a wonderful synthesis that is the essence of the Second Ray of Love-Wisdom.

Wisdom implies knowing, that is, an exact knowledge of the facts but it is also something more profound. It is not only knowing but *comprehending*. It comprehends by intuition – through a fusing with the Soul. It is the 'intelligence of heart' symbolized in Dante's Matilda, the *Loving Comprehension*.

On this theme Maurice Maeterlink has written:

> There is a great difference between saying 'this thing is reasonable' and 'this thing is wise'. At first, reason and love are in violent contrast in the Soul which is ascending, but Wisdom is born from the final conciliation of Love and Reason. And this Love is the more perfect to the degree that Reason has given way to Love. The more profound, the wiser Love becomes, the more Wisdom rises, the more it approaches Love. Love – and you will become wise; become wise and it will suit you to love. One does not truly love unless one becomes better, and to become better is to get wise.
>
> (*La Sagesse et la Destinée*)

Another function of the Second Ray is the constructive one. The First Ray puts out and formulates the proposition, the aim of the evolutionary drama and the fixing of the sublime objective. The Second Ray elaborates the Plane of Evolution, traces the life and chooses the ways. It creates the forms and the means for implementing that proposition.

It is therefore called the Great Constructor, the Geometer. (Plato called it 'God Geometrizing'). Thus, the Second Ray corresponds to the Second Person of the Trinity, the Word, Logos, Christ, the other Instructors and Saviours of Humanity (both those who come down among men to bring them light and indicate the Way of Liberation from suffering, giving comfort and encouragement, and also those Masters of the Wisdom and

Compassion who, for the love of Mankind, have made the great renunciation and have stayed to work 'behind the scenes' but in a way no less real and effective).

The Law which operates as an effect of the Ray is that of Attraction, which links, attracts and tends to unite every manifested thing. The Cross is the symbol of this Ray, both in its fundamental and cosmic union of spirit and matter, and in all the other mystical, religious and symbolic senses. The centre or chakra of the etheric body, which is the point of support of the special force and quality of the Second Ray, is the Heart. Its instrument of perception is the hearing or the Word made flesh.

Human Manifestations

One can easily deduce the human manifestations of the Second Ray from its essential qualities. The Love aspect gives the tendency to union, to inclusiveness and universality, desire in man – desire to possess, to have, even in in the egotistical sense of hoarding (especially knowledge).

It brings the yearning for material well-being, physical and emotional love, the gregarious instinct. It also brings the solitude of isolation. Its tendency to know, united to the inclusive tendency, can give place to excessive interest in details and facts – study and erudition as ends in themselves. Its ability to see many sides of a question often leads to indecision and so inaction.

Another characteristic of the Second Ray is sensitivity which, if excessive and unmanageable, can be a source of suffering and difficulty. But if it is wisely disciplined and directed, it can produce intuitive knowledge and identification.

Activities of the Second Ray

The activities in which the energies of the Second Ray are best employed are: priesthood (above all as a cure for the soul!), teaching (character formation in general) and every form of philanthropic and social service to man.

At this grave and decisive moment for humanity, when the old forms are declining and being violently broken down from their concretization, there is urgent need for the 'note' and 'quality' of the Second Ray of Love-Wisdom which helps in the building of new forms to replace the old.

It is the Ray which is stirring in the breasts of those who desire peace intensely and in whom there is a growing wish for comprehension, co-operation and unity, all in the spirit of goodwill.

8

Third Ray: Active Intelligence

The Third Ray, called the Ray of Intelligent Activity, forms a triad of major Rays with the Ray of Will and Power and the Ray of Love-Wisdom. The Third Ray is, in a sense, more evolved than the other two, and more fully manifested.

This is because it was the Ray that was prominent in the solar system preceding ours, the First solar system. The present solar system is ruled by the Second Ray of Love-Wisdom, which will become dominant only at the end of the cycle, whereas the Third Ray of Active Intelligence has matured fully during its evolutionary work.

The Third Ray represents the Divine Life as it demonstrates in every form of nature. The marvellous intelligence inherent in every particle of matter from atom to galaxy and in every organism, is the specific quality of this Ray. It is the Life of the Third Logos, the Brahma of the Indians, that pervades all.

It vivifies, evolves and transfroms all. It is the power of choice, of discrimination, that already operates in so-called inorganic matter and that reveals itself to us more openly in the minutest reactions of living material and in the surprising and complex co-ordination of cellular and organic thought.

One can say that among the functions of living things, those which demonstrate the quality of the Third Ray most aptly are the nutritive and assimilating functions which are carried out by means of the organisms' marvellous capacity for *selection*.

Every plant, for instance, knows with certainty how to choose the substances from the earth which are necessary for its vital processes. In a fuller and more general sense, the Third Ray manifests the faculty of 'riposat' and adaptation of materials and forms to the spirit, of body to soul. This renders the evolution of all things possible, not only a planet but its inhabitants.

So, although in one sense the Third Ray represents the material pole, it has also a very high and necessary function in supporting the spirit's action and renders possible the actuation of the glorious Divine Plan.

The Human Body—Masterpiece

The masterpiece of the Third Ray, operating as it does through gross matter, is the human body. A healthy body is a marvellous unity of cells, all differentiated but regrouped into organs and bodily systems which function together in perfect harmony, under control of nervous systems and endocrine glands.

In the field of the emotions, on the other hand, such order no longer exists; there is often disorder, conflict and tumult. The mind of man is in a process of development. The uncoordinated emotions and instincts frequently dominate the mind and the definition that 'man is a reasoning animal' is far from *fait accompli*! It would be more realistic to say that 'man is an animal who sometimes reasons!'

What control of the human body exists is the fruit of long and wearying practice during man's evolution in bodies born into the various Root Races over vast passages of time. By the active intervention of man's will and intelligence, the various organs of the body had to be made to work. This required constant applications of his consciousness to the physical problems of life.

At present, however, man's conscience functions predominantly at an emotive level. His interior activity and attention are turned principally towards diverse and changeable sentiments ... religion, order, harmony, peace, and many other agitated and contrasting passions.

But there is a minority of more evolved men than these, whose passions are transmuted and dominated by their attention to more intellectual activities. For long periods their sentiments and emotions are held sufficiently under control to enable them to give their attention to maintaining their consciences concentrated at mental levels where there exists the 'fire' of mind.

In the distant future, such men will arrive at a degree of development and elevation, that their trained and disciplined minds will work spontaneously, without the necessity to apply the will to their efforts.

Then man will really have become master of his three aspects—the physical body, the emotions and the mind. The resulting personality, a harmonious blending of all three, will become the co-ordinated instrument of the spiritual soul, the real and enduring part of man, who will really be a *conscious soul incarnate* and will live in the true spiritual world. On earth, the

Kingdom of God, the Fifth, will then have 'come'. It will be the event that we have constantly evoked for long ages in the Lord's Prayer, '*Thy Kingdom Come.*'

The great Spiritual Masters have given us confirmation and a living example of this glorious possibility. Christ has said: 'It is not I that lives, but my Father Who is in me.'

In Him, personality is co-ordinated and automatic. He had achieved the true impersonality. For Him, His personality life did not exist. He was really *free*. Let us keep these models in mind and aspire to them. Christ has left for us a saying that ought to have its fulfilment:

> You, therefore, must be perfect, as your heavenly Father is perfect.

Let us continue in our ascent, *the ascent of man*, towards our true possibilities, the image and true likeness of God.

The Rays and the Planes

In the highest and most perfect aspect, the Third Ray corresponds to the Third Plane or Sphere of life, called the *Atmic Plane*, which constitutes the peak of perfection of the preceding solar system or solar cycle.

In the present solar system, however, the peak of perfection is found at Monadic levels. The human monads are the highest element of the human hierarchy which is truly divine and the monad uses the soul as its instrument of expression just as, in turn, the personality is the instrument of the soul. The activity of the Divine Mind, through the monads, can reach the plane of Higher Manas, or abstract mind. Every human being possesses the elements of abstract thought, for this is the quality which differentiates him from the animal mind. The Divine Mind operates the great evolutionary plan for the earth, evolution being God's mind in action and we recognize that Presence as:

The Lord of Memory
The Interpreter of what we see
The Lord of the Balance
The Divine Separator
The Essential Discriminating Life
The Builder of the Foundations
The Procurator of Light
He who veils and unveils
The Dispenser of Time

The Lord of Space
The Universal Mind

Before examining the laws relating to the Third Ray, we shall relate firstly the various Laws operating in the world to the Rays in general:

There are three great cosmic laws:

The Law of Synthesis
The Law of Attraction
The Law of Economy

These relate to the three great Rays I, II and III. Then there is an intermediate Law which stands on its own, the Law of Karma, or Cause and Effect. Finally, there is the Group of Seven Laws of the Solar System, each one corresponding in numerical order to the seven planes of evolution. These are:

1. The Law of Vibration
2. The Law of Cohesion
3. The Law of Disintegration
4. The Law of Magnetic Dominion
5. The Law of Fixation
6. The Law of Love
7. The Law of Sacrifice and Death

If we examine the connections between all the laws and the Rays we find that:

To the First Ray corresponds the First Cosmic Law, the Law of Synthesis and also the first law of the solar system, the Law of Vibration, which is at the basis of all manifestation and originates in the First and highest Plane.

To the Second Ray is correlated the Second Cosmic Law, the Law of Attraction, and the second law of the solar system, the Law of Cohesion, which has an evident affinity with that of Attraction.

To the Third Ray there is correlated the Cosmic Law of Economy and the third law of the solar system, the Law of Disintegration. The Law of Economy governs the distribution of material atoms, their vibratory rhythm and their various qualities. The law acts so that matter always follows the line of least resistance. It produces a rotary motion. The Law of Disintegration is difficult to understand and we shall limit ourselves to noting that one of its functions is that of destruction of the forms when they have carried out their purpose and are therefore no longer suitable vehicles for Life, but rigid things that impede the Divine Plan.

The Third Ray is manifested in a predominant way in two planets of the solar system: in Saturn and the earth. In *The Secret Doctrine* the following correspondences are indicated:

Planet	Saturn
Day	Saturday
Esoteric Colour	Green
Human Principle	The Lower Mind
Divine Principle	The Universal Mind
Chakra	The Throat Centre

The Third Ray, as one would by now have guessed, qualitatively expresses the Logos of our own planet earth and, therefore, some of the correlations given above have a special meaning for our own earthly evolution.

> This Ray produces discrimination by means of mental activity, thus counterbalancing the note of Love, which is the dominant quality in the whole solar system, and this is the cause of our evolutionary development. Life enters the forms, thanks to this discriminating and selective activity, and passes from one experience to another in a wider scale of contacts.

In Humanity the Ray of Active Intelligence lies at the base of every civilization; all forms of social life, every step in technical and cultural progress, derive from it.

All the arts and sciences, all that is produced by specifically human means, all the intellectual and artistic activities derive from it and the four minor Rays which it synthesises. The means of communication between men such as transport, telephone, telegraph, radio and even means of monetary exchange such as gold and currency, are ruled by this Ray.

Correspondences between Rays and Races

According to Eastern teachings the evolution of the earth is carried out through Seven great Races (called Root-races) which succeed each other. Each of these Root-races is divided into seven sub-races, which also sub-divide and partially overlap.

At present we are in the cycle of the Fifth Race, to which the Indo-Europeans and the Americans belong, while the Chinese and Japanese belong to the Fourth Race. The Fifth Race is dominated by the Third Ray (fifth counting from the bottom or order in which the Races appear) which gives it its characteristic qualities. The men of this Race and Ray are those in whom the note of Activity reigns, who tend to realize, embody and concretely actuate ideas, feelings and impulses.

They are those who are vitally interested in civil and social manifestations, the progress of 'culture' in every sense, because they are generally rajasic, or active-dynamic and extravert.

Coming to more precise distinctions and qualitative calculations, one can say that the notes expressed by this Ray through various men differ according to the grade of evolution of each one's soul.

In men who are less mentally and spiritually developed, inferior and dissonant notes of the Ray are manifested. Thus, the activity and intelligence are used to egoistical ends. There is excessive interest in material things, over-valuation of forms, materialistic or pragmatic mentality, a tendency to cunning, deceit, profiteering, immersion in illusion, in blindness, glamour and maya.

They are often hedonists who greatly value ease, comforts, the pleasures of the senses, and of these, perhaps more than any, those of the table. This is not surprising if one remembers the connections between the Third Ray and the nutritive process.

The selective ability of plants becomes a sensitivity of the palate and the gourmet's faddiness.

On the other hand, in the more spiritually elevated men of this Ray one finds an intelligent use of the various forces for the actuation of the Divine Plan, a rhythmic and ordered activity in co-operation with the *all*.

Intelligentsia of the Planet

Ruled by the Third Ray of Active Intelligence, they truly make up the *Intelligentsia of the planet*. Their greatest virtue is to be realizers, to dedicate their lives to ideal tasks. The difference between these and the former, above all, is in *motive*. It is the quality of the motive that impels them to activity. They do not judge by results, as all the world does, but they act out of right motive.

But even they, at their best, must guard against over-valuing external activity and the visible, tangible results. They must avoid the snares of activism, of excessive 'busyness' – if not of actual business! They are animated by the best intentions. They must, in short, overcome their tendency to give too much importance to appearance, to form; attributing to the form a value in itself.

They must not lose sight, in the form of what is only a means of uncovering significance and value, of the underlying reality behind the form. They must, accordingly, learn to recognize spiritual realities, the power of the silent radiation, the action of inaction.

From this we may interpret a warning and a principle which can be of great value in understanding the Ray psychology. No Ray is complete and perfect when it operates separately from the others. As the First and Second Rays need the Third in order to manifest themselves objectively, they also need other Rays to effect their dignity and spiritual significance.

Only in their harmonized integration and fusion is the *divine will* actuated and man becomes a conscious and perfect 'collaborator with God.'

> He who knows the microcosm cannot long remain ignorant of the macrocosm. This is why the Egyptians, those zealous investigators of nature, so often said: MAN KNOW THYSELF. But their disciples, the Greeks, of lesser insight, took that adage as being allegorical and in their ignorance inscribed it on their temples. But I declare to you, whoever you may be, who desire to plunge into the depths of Nature, that if that which you seek YOU DO NOT FIND WITHIN YOURSELF, YOU WILL NEVER FIND IT WITHOUT. He who aspires to a first place in the ranks of Nature's students, will never find a vaster or better subject of study than he himself presents. Therefore, following in this the example of the Egyptians, I repeat their very words: 'O man, know thyself, for the treasure of treasures is entombed with you.'
>
> Alipili

9
Significance of Precious Stones

All life comes forth from God; but it comes from Him through different channels. We read in the book of Revelations of the seven spirits which are before His throne, but we learn little there of their functions.

Students of the inner life are aware that these seven great ministers are very much more than mere servants or messengers; they are rather, as it were, God's very members in and through whom He works, or, as it were, channels of His power – part of Himself – functioning under Him, somewhat as in the human body subordinate ganglia function under the control of the brain.

The divine life pours forth through these seven ministers and it is coloured by the channel through which it passes; during all its long evolution it bears the stamp of one or another of these mighty spirits; it is always life of that type and of no other whether it be at the mineral, vegetable, animal or human stage of its development.

Hence it follows that these seven types are to be found among men; that we ourselves must belong to one or another of them. Fundamental differences of this sort in the human race have always been recognized; a century ago men were described as of the lymphatic or the sanguine type, the vital or the phlegmatic, and astrologers classify us under the names of the planets as Jupiter men, Mars men, and so on.

I take it that these are only other methods of stating the basic differences of disposition due to the channel through which we happen to have come forth or, rather, through which it was ordained that we should come forth.

As these types exist among us, it is obvious that the divine force will act upon us in different ways; its incidence, as it were, will be at different angles. We are directed by Christ's Church to make certain arrangements for the reception of that force ...

The Rays run through all nature so that just as there are men belonging to each, so are there animals, vegetables and minerals belonging to each and possessing the special characteristics of that to which they belong.

We find, for example, that each Ray has its own representative precious stone, or group of precious stones, through which its force will work more readily than through any other. The following list of stones peculiar to the Seven Rays, and the subsequent remarks concerning them, are taken from *The Science of the Sacraments* by C.W. Leadbeater.

Ray	**Stone**	**Substitutes**
1	Diamond	Rock Crystal
2	Sapphire	Lapis-Lazuli, Turquoise, Sodalite
3	Emerald	Aquamarine, Jade, Malachite
4	Jasper	Chalcedony, Agate, Serpentine
5	Topaz	Citrine, Steatite
6	Ruby	Tourmaline, Garnet, Cornelian, Carbuncle, Thulite, Rhodonite
7	Amethyst	Porphyry, Violan

It must not be assumed that it is an exhaustive list, because all precious stones are on one or other of the Rays. These which I have given in the first column stand at the head of their respective Rays in the mineral kingdom, and so are their most appropriate representatives.

Why they are so, we do not yet know. It is apparently not on account of their chemical constitution, for in that respect the sapphire and the ruby are practically identical, yet the forces flowing through them are radically different.

Possibly the colour of the stone may be an important factor. Further investigation will no doubt in time clear up these points; in the mean time, the accuracy of the list, as far as it goes, may be depended upon.

In the second column I add the names of some stones of less value, which may be substituted when those in the first column are unobtainable; but the stones of this column would need to be large in size if they are to be equally effective.

10
All Is Energy

The Christian symbol of the Cross with its vertical and horizontal limbs is indicative of the descent of life into matter and wherever there is such an interplay of the two, an energy centre is formed.

The energy of life and spirit mingling with the energy of matter reinforces the basic occult principles: *There is naught but energy* and *God is life*. Add to these the principle of *energy follows thought* and we have the whole basis of Yoga as it is applied to the energy centres. These energies forming their centres are found everywhere, in the smallest vibrating atom up to the greatest pulsating galaxy. *All is energy*.

The various kingdoms have different numbers of chakras manifesting through them:

Minerals	One Chakra
Plants	Two Chakras
Animals	Three Chakras
Man	Five Chakras
Adepts	Seven Chakras

The purest Ray energies flow through the minerals, for they are not admixed with other Ray energies. Thus, in the gemstone of the *diamond* we have pure Ray I energies. Out of this arises the power of stones to treat disease conditions arising out of excessive Ray stimulation or depletion of one of the Septenary.

Thus, we can derive certain correlations:

Throat chakra: Saturn: Ray III: Emerald: Hypothyroidism.

The two chakras found in plants lie below the meristem and above the root tip of each. In these regions are to be found accretions of plant hormones and wherever there are hormones produced, or places of intense stress, there are bound to be chakras, even if they are of a minor nature.

The Muladara

In animals, all three chakras are found below the diaphragm. In all kingdoms, the chakra at the base of the spine – or Muladara – is patent. From this we may gather that the single chakra found in every mineral is the Muladara, hence its potency. Because the chakra found above the root tip of plants must also be the base of the spine, it is plain to see that roots must be very much concerned in therapy needed for those diseases related to the base of the spine or Muladara.

Thus skin disorders, Addison's disease and other afflictions related to the suprarenal glands and their chakra, the Muladara, should respond to the roots of some plants.

In the knowledge of energy and its laws lies the secret of healing, always remembering that disease is a purifying process. Disease occurs where energy is not functioning according to the laws of nature.

Man's various bodies are but concretions of energy and the sources of the energy influx must come through the chakras or force centres. Hence their importance in any study of man and his behaviour, both in health and disease.

All planes carry reservoirs of energy. The reservoir of energy on the physico-etheric plane is mainly centred around prana which finds its way into man's organs through his chakras and through the mechanism of breath. Each chakra tends to be more related to certain tissues than others.

The solar plexus chakra is related to the stomach, the liver, the pancreas and the duodenum. But there are also minor centres related to these organs *per se*. Furthermore, each large organ in the body is related to its opposite magnetic polarity in the region of the brain. If the liver is the south pole of that polarity, then its north pole is found in the head centres. Hence the susceptibility of the body part to thought ... *energy follows thought* and each man is his own best physician. Herein lies the basis of esoteric healing and that attitude of mind which supports good health and also, by its negative nature (negative polarity), encourages poor health.

Triangle of Etheric Energies

Each breast, in both male and female, is related to a chakra and these are said to form a triangle of etheric energies with another chakram that lies where the clavicles articulate with the manubrium sterni.

The sexual organs, being massive sites of hormonal production and stress, have force centres related to them.

There is an important and major centre related to the vagal fibres in the arch of the aorta and this is correlated to the thymus gland.

Wherever there are considerable streams of energy at play, there will always be etheric centres. The hands and feet qualify for this distinction more than any other body part. The joints also fall into this category. Behind the knees, in front of the elbows, and, in fact, wherever large, smooth and bony surfaces articulate, energy centres will be found. Through these centres flows the Ray vibration correlated to that centre.

Additional Notes on the Centres

Sacral Centre:
Centre of lower creative activity, controls the sex life. In the disciple this energy has to be transmuted to that of the Throat Centre. This will remain a powerful centre until two-thirds of humanity are initiated. Generative process must be maintained to provide vehicles for incoming souls.

Solar Plexus Centre:
The most active in average man at this time. Through it emotional energy of the astral plane flows. Desire Centre, the energy of which must be re-focused in the Heart Centre. Predominant during Atlantean times and produces ambition and progress at first, and aspiration for enlightenment later. Mediums working unconsciously through this centre should later, in full consciousness, arouse and use the Ajna Centre.

Base of the Spine Centre:
Really the last centre to be aroused. The centre of planetary force within man. The opposite pole to the Head Centre energy, the arousal of which causes a sparking of poles and the raising of Serpent Fire.

Heart Centre:
Brought into functioning activity after the second initiation. Its energy is magnetic and radiatory. In many it is the principal centre used in healing. Receives the upturned energies of the

Solar Plexus Centre.

Throat Centre:
Centre of creative energy as demonstrated by the present Fifth Root Race and its widespread activities. Receives energies transferred from the Sacral Centre.

Ajna Centre:
Functions after the third initiation when the personality is integrated and under direction of the soul. Seat of the Third Eye and the powers of higher clairvoyance. The healing energy of the heart *flows* out from the healer but the healing energy of the Ajna Centre is *directed* to the patient.

Head Centre:
Centre of syntheses. The home of the soul. Its arousal brings perfection. The end of the road and of rebirth.

11
The Mysteries of Colour

Music and Colour to the Mind are as Air
and Light to the Body

Plato

It is taught today that the ability to distinguish colours is peculiar to man and to the snake. There are no other creatures that possess this sensory capacity — or if they do it is very embryonic.

It is also said that this capacity came to man as a chance mutation of the gene only some few thousand years ago. Be that as it may, it is well known that colour was used by the Greeks, both in practical ways and in the symbology of their ancient rituals and mysteries.

In the mystery schools of ancient Egypt, the candidate for initiation was given the colour of his predominant Ray.

It is known esoterically that the ability to distinguish extreme subtlety of colour indicates a person who is advancing in self-unfoldment. The capacity to dream in colour is another indication of the arousal of higher centres in the etheric body. Perhaps one of the reasons why the snake was chosen as the symbol of Wisdom in biblical and other occult works is because of this power, shared with man, to interpret colour.

The correlation of colour interpretation with the development of Divine Wisdom stems directly from the occult knowledge that the nature of the soul in man is *quality*. The nature of the outer shape and form of each one of us depends, to a great extent, upon this inner quality (the soul). Man is the product of the interplay of forces streaming from the soul and from those pouring in from his environment. By *man* it is meant here both the physical body and the mind with their product the Personality.

Atma-Buddhi-Manas

From within comes streaming into the consciousness the energy forces of the spiritual triad known as Atma-Buddhi-Manas. These forces are registered by man as *quality* in the shape of colours thrown on to the 'inscape' of his consciousness and reflected into the personality and the bodies of the lower triad – mental, emotional and physical. The soul qualities may also be registered as taste, feeling, sound, will, and so on.

From without there comes streaming into the consciousness the great variety of vibrations from the environment. We call the broad inclusive band of these vibrations the electro-magnetic spectrum. Some of the vibrations are registered in the consciousness as heat, others as light, colour, sound, pain and touch.

Some are not registered at all, except through the use of accessory equipment like radio, television, etc. There are many which are missed altogether by man and his equipment. Others are camouflaged vibrations in the form of food and water.

We can see our outer body but the inner ones are normally not visible to any but a trained eye. These inner bodies are 'seen' by the clairvoyant as opalescent, ever-changing vortices of colour. The colours of such auras are not as dull as the rosy cheeks, blue eyes and flaxen hair of our physical bodies but far more brilliant.

These inner bodies feed on the energies not only of the soul, but from without, and in consuming these energies they reflect continuous change in *quality*.

A Great Radiant Sun

After millions of years of processing through incarnation, the aura becomes a great radiant sun which characterizes the Adept or perfected man, no longer bound to the wheel of rebirth. This is what Plato means when he says the mind feeds upon Music and Colour.

The energies of the soul reach right down into the etheric body and we recognize them outwardly as vitality. They give the body its beauty of action and form. The energy which we derive from without, like food and oxygen, produces activity within us rather than vitality and quality. An analogy drawn between man and plant indicates clearly man's dependence on higher energies, like sound and colour for spiritual growth.

Just as a man searches in the earlier part of his evolution in material things for his sustenance, growth and comfort, so too does the seed at first search underground with its roots for its water, nitrogen and mineral salts. Later, both man and plant draw on higher energies for the greater growth of their spiritual and more beautiful counterpart. The plant reaches above ground into sunlight for energy to build its foliage: man reaches within himself for energies and inspirations which will build a perfected being.

The plant sends out subtle parts of itself or shoots; its leaves, the higher counterparts of the roots, pick up the energies of light and oxygen in a process known as photosynthesis. Man draws, by means of his etheric centres, on the inner light and colour of the higher planes.

Finally, through the induction of light (and colour) both plant and man begin to radiate this light. The plant does it in the form of a flower (which is transmuted light) with its scent and pollen; man, as a saint, radiates his Inner Light in the qualities of virtue and positive action.

Where is there evidence that living things are sensitive to light and colour? We have just now considered plants and their reaction to light. How many of you remembered that the plant is more advanced in its development than the human kingdom, speaking relatively? In that case, we have much to learn from the plant and its activity as it nears perfection. We are concerned here with light and colour; and from the extraordinary capacity of the plant to draw on light for sustenance we are ourselves made aware that one day we, too, as we reach towards perfection, will be called upon to take in tremendous quantities of light for our growth.

Rebuilding of Atomic Substance

In the atoms of the mineral kingdom there seems to be evidence of a continuous building up and destruction and rebuilding of atomic substance as occurs with the molecules in the body tissues of plants, animals and men. In the atom we get the emission of electrons (or excretion) and their replacement from an unknown source.

When this occurs there is a flash of light at the time due to the electrons changing orbit, so the scientist says. Occultists have another reason for this manifestation of light and it is concerned with an inflow of energy from higher planes, as in man.

In the simplest forms of the animal kingdom, unicellular creatures like ameoba and paramecium react strongly to light.

The sensitivity of these cells is such that light can affect their activity and even, perhaps, their ability to live and reproduce.

The cells of larger animals and of men are not of so very different an order as those of amoeba, and they must show some reaction to light and colour, too. Recently it has been shown that the mating instinct of the animal, showing itself at the spring annually, is in some way linked to the increase of sunlight after the dull days of winter.

The action of light in this case seems to work through the cells of the pituitary gland. In any case, it has been found that in man the pituitary gland can be stimulated directly by light. In man Vitamin A is activated on the surface of the body in the cells of the skin by the action of sunlight. It seems certain, therefore, that light can affect the cells of man's body.

We have here to consider the mass action of various qualities or colour of light on all parts of man's body; not only the skin must be considered but the deeper tissues, too, and even the brain and nervous systems.

Occultly we know that the pineal gland responds to wavelengths (or colours, if you wish) which lie beyond the violet and red bands of the light spectrum. Seventy years ago Mme Blavatsky likened the pineal gland, the ventricles of the brain, to the sexual glands of the female.

Very recently it was discovered that cells of the pineal gland are very similar to those in the ovary. There is a deep mystery here, correlating the creative act of the lower triad with the creative act of the higher triad in the substance of thought forms.

Colour and the Organs of the Body

Whilst it may be difficult from a scientific point of view to justify the specific reactions of parts of the body to colour, there is no doubt of this fact in the writings of the Ancient Wisdom which supplies many key as to which parts of the body are affected by which colours. Man is himself a minor universe and a replica of the solar system in which he 'lives and moves and has his being'.

From a study of the aura of the solar system we can learn much about the action of colours on man himself, who is a minute replica of that solar aura.

It is not generally possible for men to see each others' auras, but we can all see a two-dimensional representation of the sun's aura when we split the light of the sun with a prism.

From the ancient teachings we know of the colours of this aura, which represent parts of the body of the Solar Logos. From this astrological information slowly crystallized over thousands of years we know that the colour green, for instance, is correlated to the planet Saturn and to the thyroid gland in man. Rose red is characteristic of Mars and flame red characteristic of Aries.

From a close study of the seven basic tissues of the body, which are laid down from the moment of conception, it is possible to allocate colours to the organs and their parts which are made up from these tissues. Thus we find that:

Ectoderm Tissue	-	(skin, nerves and brain), is strongly affected by red.
Mesodern Tissue	-	(muscle, blood, bone), is affected by blues, yellows, and indigos.
Endoderm Tissue	-	(linings of intestines and organs), reacts strongly to greens and violets.

Individuals with an accentuation of any of these tissues will tend to respond to the corresponding colours. It should be remembered here, though, that we are dealing purely with physical tissues and that only about ten per cent of disease is the result of imbalance in the purely physical body.

Most disease stems from causes lying in the subtler bodies of mind and emotion. Clues as to colours affecting these vehicles must therefore be examined to gain the necessary knowledge.

When Dr Kilner investigated the human aura, he described diseased cases in which it was blotched and choked in the region of the disease. This imbalance shows up through the kilner screens but it is also seen by clairvoyants.

In the aura of the sun there are similar alterations or shifts in the solar spectrum as the result of planetary movements and activity. When the planet Venus is moving towards the earth there is a shift of the sun's spectrum towards violet. When Venus recedes from the earth there is a shift towards the red.

The spectrum, as seen by us, is the result of atmospheric conditions of the earth, in part, and there is no doubt that Venus' movements – and presumably the movements of other planets – affects subtle substance of the earth and all that lives within it.

Activity of the gland which is the counterpart of Venus in man, the pituitary gland, will also affect the body and also the aura of the subtle bodies.

Rationale of Colour Treatment

Realising that the aura changes continuously with every stimulation and becomes blocked and blotchy, on occasions manifesting as disease, the whole rationale of colour treatment becomes clear.

If the aura can be reached directly with the correct colour and can be altered, there will follow balance and health in the physical body.

It is therefore of great import to know the Ray colours governing the subtle bodies. To assist a man subject to mental depression we should know the Ray of the mental body and flood him with the colour of his mental vehicle. If he is over-stimulated mentally, then the complementary colour shouls be applied. This would assist in drawing off the mental blockages. The same would apply to the emotional body.

There are various methods by which we can gain a knowledge of the Rays of a person, but these are still in a state of evolvement. A knowledge of the patient's horoscope can help considerably. Exoteric rulers of the signs in the chart indicate the Rays of the lower triad.

Esoteric planetary rulers of the signs indicate the Rays of the higher triad. By applying various colours in a series of tests on the patient we can assess the speed of his reflexes and therefore find which colour stimulates him to activity of body. Careful questioning of the subject while applying various colours will also reveal the colours affecting him most, mentally and emotionally.

This work takes time and there are many general rules which may be applied in the use of colour. Always the important principle to remember is that colour (and light) assist with the regulation of mental and emotional tone in the life of man.

Generally we are confronted with two types of individual: the one who needs stimulation to activity and the one who needs relaxation and rest.

Usually *indigo*, *lemon-yellow*, or *violet* will be found productive of *activity*, but reflexes should be tested for these.

A testing of the patient's ability to relax under the stimulation of *green*, *blue* and *violet*, in this order, will normally reveal the colour of rest.

Light blue is one of the great antiseptics of esoteric healers and lacks all the poisoning influences of antiseptic drugs.

A man who needs *red* is the anaemic type, idle, sleepy or lazy.

Hot-tempered, fiery or cholic types need a colour like *blue* to calm them. The test here is to examine the urine, the excrement, the colour of the eyeball and fingernails. For reddish hue apply *blue*, for bluish hues apply *red*.

In this respect an examination of the horoscope will reveal how the planets are placed in the elements. A person with a preponderance of fire signs will tend to react well in feverish conditions to *blue*. Perhaps earthy people will respond to *red*, airy people to *green* and watery people to *yellow*.

Just as the horoscope will reveal that particular cell salt which the native is likely to be deficient in, so too will it tend to show the colours which are deficient in the aura.

A heavily afflicted Saturn in the second house will show the need for *green* to be applied and the throat centre to be relieved or stimulated.

Colour Application in Children

To bring out the Love principle in a child who has a preponderance of Will Rays with a Second Ray soul, it would be advisable to decorate his room with *orange* hues, this colour being complementary to *indigo*, the colour of Love-Wisdom and of the Second Ray.

A child who shows introvert tendencies of extreme shyness (this is the result of a preponderance of Love Rays in the make-up) will respond to being dressed in *red*. He will begin to sport himself, perhaps to show off a little, and this will help bring him out of his shell.

Apple green reflects sympathy and understanding, and a difficult child may be wooed to one's confidence through applying this colour.

Chrome yellow is always a good colour for the stimulation of mental growth in children.

When a youngster is upset and manifesting discord in his personality, the application of discordant colours can be made as a preparation for the instilling of more harmonious colours later.

A youngster in a discordant mood may seat himself at a piano and make the keys sob with agitated notes. After a period he arises apparently refreshed and his black mood gone.

The discordancy breaks up and releases the choked disharmony in the subtle bodies and, thus freed, the child is ready for further, more harmonious, treatment, perhaps with the colour of his mental or emotional Ray.

In the months of pregnancy the mother should have very

harmonious conditions about her; the playing of music is known to stimulate soul growth and this is particularly important about the third and fourth month.

The three major colours, *red*, *blue* and *green* (blue here is really *indigo*) are powerful influences on cells which are growing and dividing at a great rate, as in the case of an embryo where in nine months a single cell, measuring one two-hundredths of an inch, is transformed into the billions of cells of the new-born baby.

At an early age, certainly no later than three years, the child should be surrounded with colour and be taught to distinguish colours from each other with increasing accuracy and discrimination. This should apply, too, with sound, taste and touch. Training of the sensory faculties should be a preliminary to kindergarten.

A child born in Leo would find conditions more equitable for growth of his various bodies in a city ruled by Leo or by a fire sign. Such a child would find Leo-ruled Johannesburg more suitable than Pisces-ruled Cape Town. He would respond mostly to the colours of Leo – *orange* and *indigo*.

Methods of Applying Colour

There are many ingenious methods of directing colour to the innermost reaches of the physical body and to the aura, which needs it usually more than the former.

Colour Breathing

The rationale of this technique is based on the occult knowledge that there are very fine particles attached to the oxygen atom in what is known as a *vitality globule*. Each of the seven particles linked by pranic energy in the vitality globule has a different colouring.

When we breathe in the vitality globules, they are dispersed to the various centres. Focusing the mind upon a particular colour when breathing in will tend to accentuate the storage of the particular 'anu' from the vitality globule in its particular centre in the etheric body.

During the activity of daily life we should draw in the colour which most stimulates us to activity and this should be done consciously several times per day.

Before resting, we should do the same with that colour which is most restful (relaxing) for us.

There is of course the application of colour directly to the body through the screening of sunlight or artificial light. Umbrellas with different coloured canopies are useful here. Bernard Shaw had a rotating summer house which always presented its windows to the sun.

Here we would tend to find that people born in airy signs of Libra, Aquarius and Gemini would respond best to 'airy treatment'.

There are some parts of the globe which are correlated to particular colours. For instance, Capricorn rules India, and is strongly polarized towards *green*, *white* and *violet*. Libra rules Durban and is also polarized towards green.

The times of the daylight hours are also important in colour use. At various times of the day certain colours are strongest. At noon *orange* and *yellow* predominate. At sunset and dawn the colours at the limits of the spectrum, the reds, violets and indigos, predominate.

In plotting the hours of the day and their relation to certain colours we can recognize the value of placing patients in sunlight when the most suitable colour is prevailing over the others.

People with a leaning towards the emotions, and those with a large number of water signs in their horoscope, will find the induction of colour through water a more suitable approach. We have seen in photographs from the de la Warr laboratories the capacity for water to hold the subtle emanations of a priest's blessings.

Water can be drenched with colour and swallowed. In a few seconds every part of the body is receiving part of the water into itself. Certainly within two minutes every cell of the body derives its share from a glass of water and sunlight. In taking showers it is possible to fix coloured globes in such a way that the water is permeated with a particular colour.

We are inclined to overlook some of the less obvious reservoirs of light. All foods are derived to a great extent from sunlight and in some foods there is a predominance of certain colours. Beetroot is the obvious reservoir of *red*. When we eat we are feeding energy of activity to the body tissues but *colour* to the aura.

Diet can affect the aura considerably. Vegetable diet will tend to stimulate and feed the higher colour centres of the aura.

There has been presented here only the very basic

considerations with regard to colour. Certain mysteries remain to be unravelled. Others require research work before they can be presented to the scientific world for incorporation into exoteric thought.

No one can deny the important part which colour is beginning to play in the world. Colour decoration of homes and factories has altered for the better only in the last two decades.

Churches are being decorated in such a way as to arouse the highest spiritual feelings; in factories drab walls are being given colour with a resulting reduction in accident rate; some medical men have had singular success in the use of colour concentration to induce anaesthetical conditions in their patients; faces, horribly scarred by accidents, have responded to the treatments of violet-coloured flashes.

All this sudden increase in colour-consciousness on the part of humanity indicates what we have been awaiting for so long — the restoration of the Mysteries. In blending the harmonies of colour, sound and fragrance lies great opportunities for the development of human awareness.

Their synthesis in the mind at a time of spiritual crises heralds the rites of initiation. The Second, Sixth and Seventh Ray ashrams are working upon the dissemination of colour awareness in man at this time.

Note

The colour of our Solar System is *indigo*.

The colour of the last Solar System was *green*.

The colour of the Solar System to come is *red*.

In the last System there were no bright colours; only *greys* and *browns*.

In the next System there will be colours yet undreamed of by man.

Each of the seven colours is subsidiary to *indigo*.

Each of the seven colours has six sub-colours.

12
Two Ray Analyses

Extracts from Ray Analysis of L.H.

Here we have a woman totally unknown to me. She was born on 22 August 1928 with her sun in Leo, ascendant in Aries and moon in Scorpio. What does Aries in the Ascendant mean in esoteric parlance? Aries means opportunities to begin new cycles, opportunities to end old cycles. It's the great sign of new phases. If you want to start something new or remedy something really amiss in your life, Aries is the sign to do it in.

Q: Let's ask this young lady at the outset how she goes about her reading habits. Do you read widely or do you not have time to read, or do you read just a single book at a time, or what?

A: I take books and keep them in every room. I even take them from room to room with me in case I have 5 minutes more to read. I read a lot, only non-fiction in the last 20 years. I am totally hypnotized by the Alice Bailey books.

COMMENT: That's very interesting. She is hypnotized by the Bailey books and the first thing that came to my mind was a person who was studying the Bailey books in South Africa. He never went anywhere without a Bailey book somewhere on his person, either on a train or out into a park at lunchtime, absolutely avaricious for all-embracing knowledge.

A: I like to synthesize this and integrate it with psychology. I have a Master's degree in that field.

Q: You like to compare:

A: I like to make it fit together.

Q: Oh, you want them to fit together, not just to compare them?

A: I know that psychology is mixed up, but I hunt for the psychology that is sound enough that I can teach.

Q: You like things soundly based. Have you ever heard me lecture before?

A: Yes, several times.

Q: What qualities about the lectures that I give attract you?

A: They are organized, directly to the point. They are entertaining, of course, but I get a great deal of information in the least time possible.

Q: You like your philosophy soundly based?

A: I think it is soundly based. Other people might not.

Q: You tend to like to have it anchored in reality ... what we call reality in this world. You can't just accept anything?

A: Oh, no. I accept all kinds of things.

Q: You accept things which have no basis at all?

A: Well ...

Q: You mean that everyone has a point of view and who are you to say that they are wrong? So you read widely. What do you do with your books?

A: I get so eager to share them that I push them off on somebody, insisting that they read them.

COMMENT: I have a friend in England who leaves *Psychic News* on the bus every month; it comforts her. She says, 'You know I do a good job like that.' I'll bet you wouldn't leave one of my books on the bus ... at $14.00.

A: I bought nearly every book you had and have already loaned some of them out.

COMMENT: There's a Second Ray here somewhere. All we have to do is track it down and find out what it is and where it is.

Q: As a child, did you go to church, what church, how and what did you retain?

A: As a child we only had to go to Sunday School occasionally and it was a laughing matter, but there was a little Bible class down the street that strongly affected me. I went there once a week.

Q: And what was the reason, the man who was giving the classes? Or the parables of Jesus, or Genesis?

A: No, it must have been the philosophy, such as that we all have a guardian angel, are always being tested, etc.

Q: You tend to like to have many things on the go in your life?

A: Yes, I do have a lot of things going.

Q: Do you feel a little uneasy if you haven't got a lot on the go?

A: Yes.

Q: Do you thing that you can be accused of being a dilettante?

A: I don't think so. I go into things very deeply once I go into them.

Q: And you have a wide range of interests?

A: Yes, I do.

Q: That's interesting. What about the colours that affect you?

A: Well, I like royal blue very much.

COMMENT: The colour of the Bailey books.

A: I love yellow.

Q: Is it a nice deep chrome buddhi yellow or an insipid lemon yellow?

A: It is a pure yellow, a light bright yellow.

Q: Do you thing that you have had many mental crises in your life?

A: One after another.

Q: So you really think that you have got a Fourth Ray mental?

A: I haven't thought about that.

COMMENT: One crisis after another, and yet she gives the impression of being a harmonious person.

Q: Are you in the middle of a crisis at the moment?

A: I think not. Things are smooth right now.

Q: Now what about your interest in art? We have had a preamble; let's get down to business now.

A: In junior high school, they told us that if we would try out for a part in the operetta we might get it, but I tried out for a part that no one else tried out for and still didn't get it. I couldn't sing but I wanted to.

COMMENT: You wanted to participate in the arts that you appreciated.

A: Yes, and I couldn't do that well.

Q: You couldn't sing? You couldn't dance?

A: I did dance but I didn't study dancing seriously.

COMMENT: So although you are appreciative of art, you haven't become equipped in that particular field.

A: That's right, so I simply listen to Beethoven nearly every day.

COMMENT: Yes, this is a good indication of a Fourth Ray.

Q: Do you think that you are introvert or extravert?

A: I appear to be extraverted; I tell people everything. However, there is always something on the inner side that doesn't come out.

Q: Were you a chatterbox when you were younger?

A: Yes.

Q: Are you still a chatterbox?

A: Yes, at times.

Q: Do you still tend to compare religions? Have you still got this trait in you? Or are you strictly dedicated to one particular philosophy?

A: Yes, because I have been on it for about 15 years. Yet I do tend to try to convince others.

Q: Who would say that this is not an introvert? I think she is very extraverted.

COMMENT: So straightway we have to say to ourselves, 'this is a Will Ray personality – a personality on Ray 1, 3, 5, or 7.' There is one Love Ray that can be quite extravert, and that is the 6th Ray; but as a personality, the 6th Ray tends to be extravert only when in comfortable, familiar surroundings where there is emotional support and response from friends, or when under the influence of alcohol. But in this case, the extraversion is with anyone and whether or not there is positive emotional response.

Q: Do you tend to manage people well?

A: Usually, with diplomacy.

Q: She is tactful, but has she all her life led people into situations? Is she the leader? (*To Launa's sister.*)

A: (*from Launa's sister*): Yes, I think she is a leader.

COMMENT: I know what the personality Ray is, but I am trying to present it for you. She is interested in a wide range of activities. She does, however, go into them in some depth. She hasn't got to be facultatively extravert or introvert, which is a characteristic of the Fifth Ray personality. And in fact, even though she would like to think she plans her life, I don't think she plans it very much. You plan your studies of course, but do you tend to fiddle in your week nights? Do you keep a diary of events?

A: I do some. The irony of this is that I teach a course on 'How to Get Control of Your Time and Your Life'.

Q: Do you attract people to you?

A: I have had real nice response to these classes and I don't want to teach for credit because I then have to teach what other people say so I teach short courses that are non-credit through the Universities.

Q: Have you had to use something more than just tact in

your life to establish things?

A: Yes.

Q: You have had to use a bit of force?

A: Yes.

Q: Do you think that you use people, with good motive of course? And situations? Or would you?

A: Let's see, that's a deep question.

COMMENT: That's a hard one to answer in public.

A: Yes, I suppose I have used people. Also, I am perfectly aware when people use me and I don't mind it.

COMMENT: And if it is toward a good end. The ends justify the means. You can write that down.

Q: Tell me something about your dream life. I am still probing personality Ray here.

A: I can turn on remembering dreams and I can turn it off. I will turn it on, write them all down, and then seem to become too absorbed, and I'll turn it off for awhile until I get more balance.

Q: I presume that you wouldn't for a moment dream in anything but colour.

A: After I found out that creative people dream in colour, I began to establish my colours in dreams.

COMMENT: Somebody asked me once, 'you mean you dream in colour?' I wouldn't dream of doing anything else. And of course it works, you know. If you organize your outer life, and you emphasize it, and that's what half of you do not do ... If you do not emphasize your esoteric qualities in your outer life, then you won't dream of them and you won't experience them inwardly. You must furnish inner space. The only way you furnish inner space is to create the furniture outwardly so strongly that it grows inwardly as well. Always have some furniture in inner space that the master can sit on ... A very important point, to have furniture in your temple for Him to occupy, to be seated on. (I remember the first experience I ever had of a master, the Master D.K., who came to me in Phillipi, one howling, windy night. In my lounge I was dozing in a chair and he was seated in front of me in a half tucked asana, one leg tucked in and the other down on the ground, which afterwards I took to be a symbol of his eastern and his western links.)

I am going to posit here a First Ray personality, a rare

phenomenon in women: 5-7 per cent. They come to be focal points. They are not like a man personality-wise. They have the distinctiveness. It's there. A man, for instance, will tend to become himself a focal point and a woman will tned to become a focal point within her family, within her home, within her class, within her village. The man tends to be individualistic enough to attract attention individually to himself wherever he is. These women frequently attract in association with something. Yes.

Now let's have a look at the emotional nature. Are you a person who understands human emotion? By that I mean when you see it in front of you, do you understand, do you comprehend? Do you feel for the person who is bawling his eyes out?

A: If I see someone crying, I often have tears, or in the movies I cry.

COMMENT: She weeps; she always weeps in the movies.

Q: Tell us about your church experiences. Have you prayed all your life?

A: As a child I used to pray very frequently. I did a great deal of church work as a group leader, etc., and then I began to teach reincarnation in the Christian Church and made my exit just about at the right moment.

COMMENT: In England we say '*Aprés nous, le déluge*': (after us, the deluge).

A: I do go to church every Sunday, but now it is to a church that is based on the ancient wisdom.

Q: Do you still pray?

A: Sometimes, although my meditative life is much more important.

Q: Have you ever had a vision of the master Jesus?

A: No.

Q: A master?

A: Only one; very, very brief.

Q: You wouldn't like to describe it?

A: It was a man, Oriental or Indian in dress, young, with a beautiful face. I ran away mentally.

Q: Have you ever had any out of the body experiences?

A: Yes.

Q: Is there any doubt, in anybody's mind that this is, despite the First Ray personality, a Sixth Ray astral body? It definitely is, and you won't get one as characteristic as that! Who weeps and, like Winston Churchill, can sympathize with people and appreciate their feelings and will even make them at home by weeping with them. It is there, yes?

Q: All right, tell me something about your physical body now.

A: As a child I was sick a lot, very weak and not strong; now I am as strong as can be. However, after intense activity with lots of people, I have to draw in. I have to get away and get in balance again.

Q: Have you got good energy resources?

A: Yes, I walk or jog two miles at 6.30 every morning and then I swim almost every day.

COMMENT: A very active person. We are going to have a bit of trouble with analysing the physical body.

Q: How do you like sunlight?

A: I like sun. I used to stay in it a lot.

Q: You were receptive to it? Have you ever done any very hard work in your life?

A: I have four boys. I thought I worked very hard, even though I had help with the house and with them. Two of them are twins.

Q: Do you think that you have performed a service to humanity in the way that you have brought them up? Have you made them something special or tried to?

A: I have tried to. I don't know about humanity.

Q: Do you think they belong to the Sixth Root Race or something?

A: I have wondered about that. My oldest son was here tonight, but had to leave at the coffee break. That's why I am willing to talk. I did talk to them often about Christ and later about esoteric wisdom. Children don't always recognize hard work done for them.

COMMENT: I had a friend named Lulu Busby. She had a car which wasn't too good. This damned thing used to peter out on the hills and boil over and I used to get the thing going again and eventually get to the top of the hill and she would thank the Father for it ... like 'the Father be praised' and all that sort of nonsense – I had done all the hard work.

PERSON GETTING RAY READING: I had a person in my car with me during the festival and she thought just in time to say a little prayer about finding us a good parking place and sure enough there was one. I began to try to squeeze into it but gave up and was backing out to find another when she said: 'Don't you dare; we prayed for this and God gave it to us and you are going to take this parking place!'

COMMENT: We are still battling with this physical body.

A: Let me add that the whole family has had to learn that I am easily hurt physically; they can just give me a quick pat and it may cause pain from the top of my head to the tip of my feet. For the same reason I have to leave very loud concerts.

COMMENT: The body is an eye.

Q: What was your complexion when you were younger? Dark haired, fair skinned?

A: No, I could tan well, light brown hair.

Q: How old are you?

A: Forty-six.

Q: Would anybody like to suggest that this is not a Seventh Ray physical body? Can you do hard work?

A: What do you call hard work?

Q: Have you ever had to lift heavy things and move them, drive a car for 14 hours, scrub floors? Do yo stand up to it?

A: No, I get exhausted.

COMMENT: Stand up for a moment.

Q: Does this look like a Third Ray physical body? No, no! It is a Seventh Ray physical body, or it is possibly a First Ray, but a First is ruled out because she can take sunlight. This could be a Second Ray physical body, but I don't get the impression of it. Are you a person who has worn things in your hair, or worn a lot of hats?

A: We wore hats when we had to wear hats in certain places.

Q: But you haven't got a passion for wearing baubles in your hair?

COMMENT FROM A MEMBER OF AUDIENCE: She is not a china doll.

COMMENT: No, she is not a china doll. Would anybody like to suggest any other possible physical body than that one? I don't think you can.

Now we have got to go into the nature of the soul and, of course, this might upset everything. Tell me something about your interest in history.

A: Not very much ... perhaps ancient Egyptian mythology

and history.

COMMENT: What Ray would you put the Egyptian culture down as? Of course, Egypt was spread out over a hundred thousand years. The pyramids were built 60,000 years ago, and we don't fall for all this nonsense about Egypt being in her heyday about 4,000 B.C. Egypt was in her heyday 50,000 to 60,000 or 70,000 years ago. It was a bastard offshoot of Egypt which was in its 'heyday' 5,000 years ago. That may well be, but it is nonsense to say that you could give the Rays of Egypt, because you would have to say which part of the Egyptian civilization. It was a remnant of Atlantis. There isn't particularly a love of history here ... a feeling for Egypt which could be a Fourth Ray thing for the art of Egypt.

Q: What about archeology?

A: I would listen to a lecture; but I wouldn't read a book on it.

Q: What about poetry? Have you been concerned with poetry?

A: I was an English Literature major on my first degree but I didn't read poetry with much zest.

Q: Why do you think you are here on earth?

A: There is of course a purpose for everyone. I think my purpose is definitely in teaching and counselling.

Q: And you think it's the sort of teaching that can help people to express themselves and therefore really to heal as well?

A: Yes, particularly in the emotional body. I like to help people to understand their anger and self-pity, and to learn to laugh about these emotions.

Q: What are the predominant Rays of Leo? First, Second and a little Third. What are the predominant Rays of Aries? First, yes, and some Seventh as well.

I am going to go a little further and ask you a question that is quite important here. If you came back into life, what would you do? If you could choose your parents, your background, everything? Your family, your wealth, what would you do with your life?

A: I would do it more or less just exactly as it is right now. I would like to pick it up where I have got it right now.

COMMENT: Oh, who wouldn't!

A: I would immediately work on the mental concepts of synthesizing psychology with the ancient wisdom, using modern terminology.

Q: Did you have a change of focus, orientation, personality, three or four years ago?

A: It seems like I have gone through a number of changes, but an immense change about 10 or 12 years ago.

COMMENT: It's very rare for a woman to produce a First Ray personality in the twenties. It generally comes in the late thirties, even later still than that. It can come in the late fifties and sixties, but very rarely in the twenties and it's not very hard therefore to say there has been a change in the personality 10 years ago.

Q: Have you felt as the years have gone by, that you have gradually begun to understand life and to enjoy it and to take possession of things?

A: Yes, definitely.

COMMENT: That means that you probably have Saturn benignly in the horoscope.

A: Saturn is in Sagittarius.

COMMENT: The esoteric ruler of Sagittariusis Earth and Saturn is Third Ray and the Earth is Third Ray, and she gradually takes command of everything earthly in the sense that you are at home on the planet. First Ray souls are never at home on the planet. They always feel slightly alienated. Who in the audience would like to testify to that? Yes, I feel completely at home on the planet, as if I had a damned good hand in fashioning it. I would then put a First Ray personality here. I have done it fairly cursorily, because I would like for you all to take a part in it.

I have felt that the weakest analysis that I have done so far is of the mind; possibly a Third Ray mind here. It is a mind that, she admits herself, she has had to change tremendously. It has had crisis in it, and I don't get a Second Ray mind from this. There's a love of books and learning, but she doesn't give me the impression of being a scholar.

A: Let me add this that may help. It is strange to me. Even for a recipe for cooking, I will look up five recipes for the same dish, and then I will take the best of each one.

COMMENT: Now remember she looks up five recipes instead of one. She doesn't scatter her intentions, because her basic idea is to cook the food. She carries it through. The first thing that comes to your mind here is that this is a Third Ray mind, but she is practising what is known as an eclectic approach.

A: And I do this on lectures, too, using 13 authors, when I prepare them.

COMMENT: And you will take it and sieve it out and say: 'Now what do *I* think? What combination is the most truthful?' Now that is a First Ray personality. Quite contrary to current opinions about First Ray personalities, they are very careful people. They are careful in a way that staggers people. Observers will say you could have gone in and done it just like this. But they think very carefully and use the eclectic approach because it uses the brains of others or the material of other people's hard labour. And quite rightly so because they will brood and ponder on it and say, 'this is right; this is the best version.' Now that's the eclectic approach which is typically First Ray.

Now what about some quesitons from the audience?

Q: Do you really go into these things and how long do you stay with them?

A: I go totally into a thing when I am interested and stay with it until I wear it out. This esoteric wisdom study I have now been into about 12 years.

COMMENT: Why haven't I given the good lady a Third Ray mental body? Because Second Ray souls almost never have a Third Ray mentality, almost never. Now that is something you would never be taught in Ray classes. It is just something that has emerged with me from 20 years of experience. I know that it is extremely rare. You can look through all the Bailey teachings and mine as well and you will never find a Second Ray soul with a Third Ray mind. In fact the Third Ray mental body is 7 per cent anyway, and the 7 per cent is usually with a First Ray soul. It tends to be the same for both men and women.

The Third Ray is certainly true of counselling; it is certainly true of comparative religion and comparative philosophy, but although you started out talking about comparative things, you are really interested in something more than that. You are really looking at a thing eclectically to compare all the things together and get something that is right. Yes, I knew that right from the beginning. Well, I think that was an unusual one, a First Ray personality in a woman.

Q: How do you rule out the Fifth Ray mind?

A: Well, there was this attitude of stress, constant stress. There was a love of artistic things, not certain that her philosophy should be factually based. She said it didn't really matter, she had gone into all sorts of philosophies that had no factual basis at all. She is a busy woman; she must be if she has four children. Naturally she would have to plan her life, but I didn't get the impression from her that she is a planner all the time. She uses the First Ray approach of *using*.

Q: Are First Ray personalities pushy?

A: Yes, I didn't ask you if you were pushy.

A: My husband says I am.

COMMENT: Yes, they are. Any more questions? You should also notice that First Ray personalities can be quite unexpected. They don't throw themselves around all the time, as it were. She gives me the impression also of being persistent, don't you think? She is persistent with everything she does, and I rather think that it isn't interest in the subject that makes her go deeply into it. It is the persistence she gives to the thing. She persists through to the end. They can be damned persistent people and unremittently persistent.

A: By your enemies that is called stubborn.

COMMENT: Yes, and there is no doubt she has got energy and yet she can't really drive the physical body; she would have been much better to have been far more robust in the sense of being larger in frame. I think that you wouldn't have had that delicate nature you had when you were younger if you had had the Third Ray physical. And I didn't ask about gynaecological problems, which are indicative of the Third Ray physical. When you are not quite sure about whether it is the Seventh Ray or the Third Ray physical, go into the gynaecological problems. It is not necessary here.

Q: Where does the great desire to teach come in? On the Second Ray soul?

A: Yes, and she has skirmished a lot before she found what she really wants to do. I think she is not absolutely certain now that she has found her vocation. I venture to say that you will probably change direction again. You won't be really satisfied until you can start teaching the esoteric.

Q: How do you describe what she is searching for? Wouldn't it be for what seemed to be the Truth?

COMMENT: I would suggest here that she definitely find time to get more meditation in which would make her receptive of her own teachings rather than having to be eclectic. If you were to meditate much more and lead a more subjective life you would find that your own teaching would stream through. I would say, '*Go on, get out into the world and for heaven's sake remember that we are very, very few. Go and teach the esoteric. I think that's what we should all do, to go out and express the soul!*' And a Second Ray soul loves a First Ray personality. I would suggest the three great truths for her. They are in the opening page of *The Jewel In The Lotus*. It comes from *The Idyll Of The White Lotus*:

> Hear me, my brother. There are three truths which are absolute and cannot be lost, but yet remain silent for lack of speech. The soul of man is immortal; its future is the future of a thing whose growth and splendour has no limit. The principle which gives life dwells in us and without us, is undying and eternally beneficient. It is not heard, or seen or smelt but is perceived by the man who desires perception. Each man is his own absolute lawgiver, the dispenser of glory or gloom to himself, the decreer of his life, his reward, his punishment. These truths which are as great as life itself, are as simple as the simplest mind of man. Feed the hungry with them.

That is my advice to this First Ray personality. You have got it; now go out and do it – *go out and do it*!

There follows the Ray formula of L.H. It indicates an extravert:-

			4
Rays	II	1	6
			7

Case History and
extracts from Ray Analysis of K.N.

1949: 7 November – Sister born.

1950: Concept of God: Mist so fine we are unable to perceive it; 'Where is God?' asked to parents: answer, God is everywhere.
Wanted a horse since age 3; difficult to understand why I'd been born at a time when one didn't ride a horse to school.

Raised in Methodist church; religiously, parents very conventional.

Father was in Air Force Reserves after World War II; was recalled in Korean War; we moved to southern Maine on the coast; very lonely for my mother in the country.

1951: We moved to the Air Force base in Manchester, New Hampshire. Neighbourhood kids were tough. Mother saw me very close to a child ... she couldn't leave my little sister, but finally saw the child had a knife pointed at my stomach, but I wouldn't back down.

1952: We returned to our house in Tyler; my father and his business partner were starting an insurance adjusters' firm ... really started before we went to Maine.

Life was good ... lots of friends.

Always attended church; parents very active in church. Always were personal friends with minister and family.

1953: Started school, very easy, lots of friends.

Had first swimming lessons ... too uncomfortable in water to be in group lesson; had the first of several years of private lessons.

Got along with everyone except my mother; this relationship problem with my mother existed until recently. We understand each other better since I've grown.

1954: Life still very good. Began piano lessons.

1955: Few health problems ... was almost completely deaf from enlarged adenoids before it was discovered; sister had same problem at same time; adenoids and tonsils removed; I had urinary infections and numerous bladder dilations; first time to have severe headaches. Once thought to be all migrained; now very few and most of the few are sinus.

1956: School still easy ... really remained so until last year of college.

Took first family vacation, and from then until end of high school these trips continued every year; covered most states, southern Canada, and parts of Mexico in to Mexico City.

Dream: Only I exist; I created two worlds which were enclosed in a bubble coming from my forehead; I focus on one of the worlds and observe and determine what people do.

1957-58: Life very good.

1959: Entered junior high school; from this point until end of high school, I never really fit in my environment.
Discovered to have underactive thyroid.
Extreme menstrual cramps until age 25.
Only time to be anything like happy was at the farm with my father where we had horses, bought the preceding Christmas.

1960: Finished schooling (junior and senior high).

1965: Mother continued to make me feel like a failure.
Age 16 ... repeat of bladder problems, causing end of piano lessons since I was out of school so much.
Being in the country continued to be my escape.
Was an avid reader, as always in my life.
Worked in a Head Start School under a black teacher with all black children and enjoyed it.
Fall – left home to go to college.
College selection based on these factors:

1. Mother determined I would have to return home as a failure (not academic enough) at mid-term ... so must be a state school to save transportation costs.
2. Large state school far enough away to prevent casual visits by parents (425 miles from home).
3. Cooler climate which was better for my headaches.

College was difficult and many others found it the same. They confided in me, which allowed me to push my troubles into the background.

1966: Spring ... ready to transfer to another school. Decided to run for President of freshman scholastic honorary: if I got it, I would stay, otherwise I would change – I won.
Summer ... I had been accepted as a summer exchange to live with a Danish family even though my mother wrote of my self-analysis; it was a fantastic experience and I still keep in touch with the family at Christmas; my parents moved to San Antonio, Texas.

1967: Through my freshman and sophomore years, much mental unrest; often thought of suicide ... didn't seem to have anything to live for.
Spring ... at a leadership retreat I met the guy I almost married; from the first day I felt I knew everything about him ... except for one thing.
For my summer vacation I visited relatives in San Juan,

Puerto Rico.
Just before the end of the year, we decided our life styles were too different ... the tremendous feelings of love we had will always be with me in terms of an example of what love can be.

1968: Mental problems which had melted away returned; looking back I see I have a grand set of friends who kept me going.
Sister and I went to summer school in Mexico City.
Father dies 31 July while we were in Mexico; he had never been sick and it was quite unexpected; as far as I know the death certificate says 'natural causes'.
He was found asleep in a chair at the farm.
My 21st birthday was spent at a horse auction where we took my colt. He was really scared and I stayed in the heat with him almost to the point of heat exhaustion.
We sold remainder of horses. I spent rest of summer exercising skittish horses.
With my father's death, my world really fell apart; as a family, he had been the centre of the wheel.
Christmas was spent in California with relatives; on the way I spent a week in Tucson, Arizona, where my last year's boyfriend was; love still was there, but we wouldn't marry.

1969: My college days ended in May; through to the end, I continued with great depressions; my life wasn't important – spent a week in June in Mexico City.
Started work with IBM as a computer operator. I moved from Lubbock, Texas (college town) to Dallas.
I lived in an apartment for the first time, by myself.

1970: Mother and I went to Europe ... travelled through parts of Germany, Denmark, Switzerland, and Austria.
Job changed ... IBM sent me to basic computer training.
I was a trainee systems representative ... didn't make many friends ... very lonely.
One friend, as mentally mixed up as me, kept me under his control though neither of us realized that's what it was. He and his wife wanted me to move in with them, but I didn't.

1971: Continued increasing job skills.
Went with friends to Hawaii for vacation.
Moved to another apartment ... room-mate was someone

I didn't know. I had to be her mother.
Moved again ... in with college friends, when one got married and a vacancy occurred (two room-mates).
Enjoyed living with them.
Through these years I dated numerous boys who were ready to marry me or to sleep with me, neither of which I was ready for.

1972: IBM changed my job to another office – more account assignments – in utilites industry.
Went skiing for the first time and broke left leg and tore knee ligaments. This happened in November but I was on crutches throughout February, the cast being on my leg only three weeks.
By then I had moved again when one room-mate married; room-mate lived with her boyfriend so I was really by myself.
In the summer I went on a tour with one room-mate to Europe – London, Paris, Denmark; great trip.
My job assignment during this year was much too hard and most weeks were 100-plus hours at work in order to make sure I wouldn't be fired. I worked on a contract and spent many extra hours in self-education since the customer shouldn't pay for my lack of knowledge.
This year was spent on the contract at the Federal Reserve Bank.

1973: Continued at the Fed. until April; moved to another bank, where I still am assigned today. IBM usually assigns people in my job function to only one account if it is large. I specialize in teleprocessing and data base structures. I have correlated the physical data base to a 'physical life' and logical data base to multiple or all 'physical lives' of an entity; sometimes with regard to an update in a logical structure, more than one physical structure is updated ... this seems to be true also in the relationship of one physical life to another.
In July I was sent to Los Angeles to class. IBM continuously updated employees with new technology and we are in school several times a year.
My L.A. room-mate suggested I read *Many Mansions*. This was the introduction to me of the entirely different framework of reference which I use today.

School lasted 5 weeks, home for 2, then to San Jose for 3 weeks of school.
September ... began TM form of meditation, and life has changed phenomenally since then.

1974: Attended ARE: Association for Research and Enlightenment. Original group I was attracted to was newly formed and during a few months I found they had goals more oriented to being a power source for revelation than usual ARE study; in March I left.
Before joining ARE I attended a TM weekend retreat which resulted in my discontinuing with TM. In joining ARE I changed to an affirmation or other focus in meditation.
Joined another ARE group; during these months I learned plenty and met many karmic associations.
Joined a Kung Fu class oriented to meditation and slow moving forms which lasted 9 months.
Attended several metaphysical churches but didn't really find a niche.
All in all, the best year of my life to that point.

1975: When Jonathan Stone began evening services at Unity, I returned there, having discontinued ARE.
I really feel at home with the people at Unity and the Awareness Centre.
Continued my volunteer work started in November '74 at Parkland County Hospital in the Emergency Room; I had wanted to take nursing training at night and found it not available ... did volunteer work instead ... *very* informative and I enjoyed helping people.
Attended Dr Baker's seminar in May ... many new doors opened.
Spent 3 weeks in May working for IBM in Hong Kong.
Spent 2 weeks in India on vacation, plus a few days in Athens; the total trip was wonderful; people everywhere could not do enough for me and many gave me presents.
Spent 4 days immediately on return at an IBM seminar in Miami where I was reminded of all the work associations I've built across the U.S. during my employment.
Attended parts of the Yoga and Esoteric Sciences Festival.

Each day, each minute is precious to me now. I truly love life. Without my periods of mental crisis, I wouldn't have spent so much time questioning myself and analyzing myself. Now I need to learn even more of myself and the universe, but I am glad for the introspection of the past. If I had been a more mature child, I would have realized that my mother was also still a child ... crying and going to her room without speaking. Today, she has arthritis and takes much medicine, including cortisone.

My sister married last April to someone I like.

My current interests are photography, tennis, horseback riding, sailing, playing the piano (I bought a piano last April), reading, crewel sewing, great art appreciator of more forms and non-forms, being outside to be with nature. The goal of progressing on the path is not to be confused with interests.

The only time my physical body was in danger involved a saddle slipping under the stomach of my colt. I fell so that my head was under his front feet and my feet were near his hind feet. Everything went into slow motion, I had no feeling of fear, and had plenty of 'time' to move as his feet frantically moved.

Many of my friends now think they know me, but they don't. An example was that last fall I became a friend of a guy who had spent 7 years in prison for a double homicide. He and I both grew through the relationship as he readjusted. There'd definitely been a soul recognition with him. This association confounded even the girl and her twin who initially gave me *Many Mansions*.

My sister and I are very good friends and I am very lucky to have been in the same family with her. She is currently writing her thesis in government on prison reform and this fall will teach her own course at University of Texas at Austin.

Questions asked in Reading

1. Importance of church:
   Profound effect on early childhood; after puberty, not so much. In looking back, effect probably deeper that I realize.
   College years – attended different churches in search for one where I fit. Episcopalian was the best, but something was still missing.
   I relate to Jesus, but more likely to relate to the nameless

One. Sometimes in prayer I use 'God'.
Meditation is very natural.
I meditate more than pray.

2. I easily shoulder responsibility.
3. Do I underrate myself:
   Most of my life, yes.
   Now I am working to change and have a much better self-image.
4. I am fairly good at organizing.
5. Detail *v.* general: I can do either, not preferring one over the other. Must understand general in order to detail.
6. Qualities of Dr Baker's lectures that appeal to me: content, on so many levels. I tend towards mystical side, may need to balance a bit towards scientific.
7. Subjects I liked in school were maths and history.
8. I read a book from page 1 to end; I read 10 at same time.
9. I am emotionally stirred by living vicariously through book and movie characters; increasing interest in ancient civilizations.
10. Why am I here? I don't know (soul's purpose?).
11. Came back to work out karma, learn and experience more.
12. What would I choose for my next life? Since I don't know what experiences I need to reach self-realization, I can't specify; with a goal of union with the Nameless One for myself and the entire planet, I would choose what would further the progress on that path the most (if I knew). I feel drawn to help people and animals in the best way I can now and would continue to do so in the coming ages.
13. Poetry – always liked it; now interpret much better.
14. Introvert as a personality.
15. No spiritual experiences; many vivid dreams. Sometimes easy to think dreams are reality.
16. Rarely lose temper; can't think of a reason for doing so.
17. Some people think of me as cold emotionally.
18. Never been devoted to anyone.
19. Lots of mental crisis; definitely grown from it.
20. Some things I would never share with a person.
21. I can stand lots of sun in summer, but am very fair in winter. I get windburn in winter only.
22. My diet is vegetarian.
23. Emotional nature: people confide in me and I learn from it. Interactions with all people cause a learning experience.

24. Never wear anything in hair; no hats.
25. Maximum I have weighed is 130, currently 115 lbs.
26. Never done really hard work ... can do hard work short periods – dig fence post holes, build barns. Never asked to do anything for extended time.

The Ray formula of K.N. (denoting an introvert) is:

$$\text{Rays I} \quad 2 \quad \begin{cases} 4 \\ 2 \\ 3 \end{cases}$$

An efficient esoteric psychologist can deduce more than a hundred character qualities from a Ray formula.

APPENDIX

First Ray Virtues
Courage to persist against all odds...
Certain knowledge of his destiny and ultimate success, and the confidence that goes with this...
The ability to set afire those about with the same zeal and enthusiasm.
The ability to blend mercy with justice...
Loyalty to the Master and the capacity to shoulder blame for his occult superiors...
To work alone, unpraised and unsupported...
To make large decisions unaided and snap judgements that are fair if not always wise...
The ability to handle both the strong and the weak in men and in situations...

First Ray Vices
A pride that will brook no criticism...
An ambition that knows no bounds...'*Better to reign in Hell than serve in Heaven'*...
A wilfulness that knows no reason...
An anger, when aroused, that bears no placating...
An arrogance that cannot be bridled...
An obstinacy that survives all persuasion and punishment.

The Second Ray Astral Body
The Second Ray astral body is always calm and unruffled. It dislikes displays of emotion. Husbands may sometimes think them cold fish. They carry love with them everywhere they go but it is a discriminating and well-disciplined love. When criticised, their first consideration is for the person who levelled the criticism and that he be thanked for his concern. They hoard books and always keep a library from which they will lend out their books to the group.

The Second Ray Physical Body
This is a rarity perhaps with an incidence at this time of two per cent of the population. It is characterised by a small and lightly built frame. The skin is soft and women of this type are like china dolls. They are short in stature and there is a degree of vanity. The hair is often built high on the head and excessive attention is paid to it. Frequently things are worn in the hair decoratively. Older students will remember perhaps the typical form of Carmen Miranda in her hey-day. Generally the physical body is a vehicle for a Second Ray soul and there is strong rapport with it to the extent of conscious mediumship but never unconscious.

The Fifth Ray Personality

Facultatively able to be extrovert or introvert as the occasion demands. (*'Left to one's choice, optional; giving the power of doing or not doing something or assuming or not assuming a character.'* —The World Book Dictionary.)
May use (or abuse people) with or without high motive.
Careful planning of the daily activities well ahead.
Evenings filled usefully.
Constantly analysing people or situations about them.
Critical, analytical, separative and over-discriminating in practice.
Lucid but often interminable explanations for their actions.

The Fifth Ray Mental Body

The mental qualities of those listed above.
In books, there is an interest in science-fiction.
Extremely sensitive to matters which involve perception of the truth, in themselves or in their environment.
Read books for a purpose, underline, mark them, extract from them.
Like their philosophies, no matter how nebulous, to have some sort of foundation, that can be checked against scientific facts.
Critical, analytical, separative and over-discriminating in thoughts.
The mind is unremittent, will not let a thing lie until every aspect of it has been thoroughly investigated and dealt with.
Pursues the frayed edge of some problem to its ultimate resolution, rubbing salt into open wounds (of those about him) until the bitter end.
He is like the barber that snips and snips, long after it seems to all but him that the job is done.
Artistic appreciation is there but it is secondary to strict accuracy.

The Sixth Ray Astral Body

The qualities of this vehicle are so well-known that they need only be listed:

Frequently resort to prayer, especially to Jesus.
Have dreams that are often related to the object of their devotion... such as the Master, guru or some hero or father figure.
Preference for colour blue or rose.
Selfish and jealous love.
Are unable to express their powerful energies unless they are emotionally involved in the project.
Numerous prejudices, superstitions, and parallelling these and caused by them, usually a powerful astral dweller.

Out-of-body experiences.
Resolve their problems by intuitive 'reasoning' rather than analytical.
Come to quick conclusions and decisions which they often credit to some higher authority, thus giving them the emotional drive to implement the decisions.
Generous only in directions which are specifically related to the object of their devotion and exclusive to all others.
Lacking in common sense. Unable to 'reason' unless they are dealing with the problem emotionally. This often results in appalling errors of judgement of people and situations. The quick salve to all their faults is prayer for redemption.
They dislike violence but when aroused (in the defence of the ideal or to further it) they fight like demons possessed.
Capable of opposites concurrently. For example, they can be extremely pure in intent, and even in practice, and yet, descend to the depths of depravity in isolated episodes which are explained away as momentary intrusions of 'the devil'.

ECTOMORPH

Typical of the First Ray Physical Body

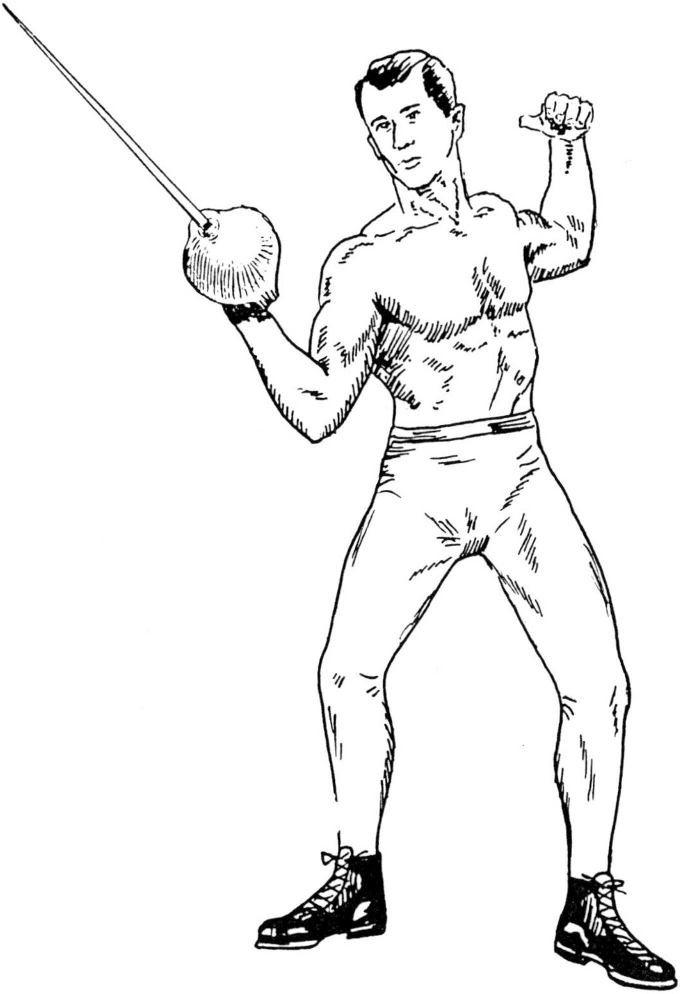

MESOMORPH

Typical of the Third Ray Physical Body
in early manhood

ENDOMORPH

Typical of the Sixth Ray Physical Body

MESO - ECTO

Typical of the Seventh Ray Physical Body

Claregate College (EST. 1973)

Director of Studies: Dr. Douglas M. Baker, B.A., M.R.C.S., L.R.C.P.

Correspondence Course

Diploma of Metaphysics

With the approach of the New Age, man's mind is rapidly expanding; vast new concerns present themselves. The normal academic education does not provide solutions to most of the problems of the incoming age. Claregate College answers five great questions: *Who are we? Where do we come from? Why are we here? Where do we go from here?* and *Why must we suffer pain?* In response to these questions, the diploma course in metaphysics is offered.

This well-established course is calculated to equip the student with a thorough understanding of the Wisdom of the Ages, as it has been practised in ancient cultures, and also as it is applied to the problems of living in the world today. With the knowledge provided and the techniques suggested, the student becomes well grounded in the vast range of theories and practises that form the basis of metaphysics.

Four main subjects are covered by the course:

* Esoteric Science
* Esoteric Healing
* Esoteric Psychology
* Esoteric Astrology

This course, designed to be relevant to the stresses of modern living, is unrivalled in its presentation of the Ancient Wisdom in the language of the day. The format provides a sound and stable foundation for creative living. Enrolled students who have followed other approaches remarked how *this* course synthesized and clarified their previous studies.

COURSE STRUCTURE: The material for the course consists of 24 lessons, each containing 2 cassette tapes, written material, drawings, question sheet, work project and required reading from the textbooks. Each lesson is designed to take one month to complete, but students wishing to take longer may do so. No educational qualifications are required. Minimum age 21 years.

FEES: The initial registration fee to enrol in the correspondence course is £50, which covers tutorial and administrative requirements and is non-refundable. The fee thereafter is only £25 per month per course packet. In addition, students are expected to purchase the course textbooks as required.

Please write for enrolment form to:

The Registrar, Little Elephant, High Road, Essendon, Herts., AL9 6HR